MEDICAL MENTORS

PRACTICING THE ART OF MEDICINE IN DULUTH 1927-1996

MEDICAL MENTORS

PRACTICING THE ART OF MEDICINE IN DULUTH 1927-1996

KATHLEEN HANNAN

Pfeifer-Hamilton
Duluth, Minnesota

Pfeifer-Hamilton Publishers
210 West Michigan
Duluth, MN 55802-1908

218-727-0500
http://www.wholeperson.com/~books
E-mail: phbooks@wholeperson.com

Medical Mentors: Practicing the Art of Medicine in Duluth 1927–1996

Printed in the United States of America

10 9 8 7 6 5 4 3 2 1

Editorial Director: Susan Gustafson
Manuscript Editor: Kathy DeArmond-Lundblad
Art Director: Joy Morgan Dey
Graphic Design: Jeff Brownell

Library of Congress Catalog Card Number: 96-61699
ISBN 1-57025-148-7

To Bob, whose endless patience and good humor
are only exceeded by the one quality I appreciate more—
he actually likes the computer.

Contents

FOREWORD

Ten years ago, we founded Pfeifer-Hamilton Publishers specifically to celebrate in print the natural beauty and the remarkable people that make Northeastern Minnesota such a special place to live. When Kathleen Hannan brought us a manuscript celebrating the lives and service of forty-four prominent retired Duluth physicians, we knew immediately that this book fit our mission.

Being a physician is more than a profession; it is a lifelong commitment to service. Physicians have always played an integral role in the fabric of community. They care for our families, heal our physical ills, calm our fears, offer wise guidance, and provide emotional support during times of crisis. The family doctor is advisor, healer, and witness to the key events of our lives.

We met many of these dedicated physicians in their role as teacher, generously and patiently passing on their passion and wisdom, year after year, to a parade of medical students, interns, and residents who came to Duluth for topnotch medical education. Nearly every doctor practicing in our region today was fortunate to have several of these gifted physicians as teachers and mentors.

Duluth's outstanding reputation as a regional medical center has grown from the efforts of these pioneers, who practiced medicine in our midst when it was as much an art as a science. Together, they represent almost two thousand years of cumulative service and somewhere around a million patient-care visits. We owe a deep debt of gratitude to these remarkable men and women, who have worked, quite literally, day and night to keep us healthy.

Here are their own reflections on their professions and their lives. In spite of crowded schedules, mountains of paperwork, long hours, and the awesome responsibility they shouldered, most would do it all over again. Elizabeth Bagley warmly sums up their feelings by saying, "My patients were no trouble at all."

These pillars of our community have taught us how to live well and have inspired the current generation of physicians to carry on their tradition of service. We are proud to publish this volume that celebrates Duluth's medical mentors and offers you a glimpse of their lives of service and their wisdom. Their legacy continues to benefit us all.

Donald A. Tubesing   Nancy Loving Tubesing
October, 1996

INTRODUCTION

I love history. I always have. There is something about the movement of humanity as it passes through time that fascinates me. The error inherent in historical study is to believe that it comprises only events on a huge scale. In fact, history is carried along quietly, often heroically, sometimes foolishly, by people like the people we all are—workers, families, loners, teachers, joiners, poets. For good or not, we all play a part in history, and to ignore our place in it is to lose our only chance to improve upon it. We can't invent the printing press, discover electricity, or walk on the moon. But we can celebrate history where we find it—all around us, where we least expect it.

In order to better understand historical trends in medicine as practiced in the Duluth area over the last seventy years, I interviewed forty-four retired physicians, asking each a similar set of questions—When did you first realize you were interested in medicine? How did you decide to settle in Duluth? In your opinion, what one development most affected the way you practiced medicine? Was there a case so unusual you still remember it today? What advice, based on your years of practice, would you give a physician just beginning his or her career? In this book, I have recorded their responses to these questions in their own words—edited for length but not for content. Some of the doctors spoke philosophically; others focused on practical issues. Together, their statements describe an exciting era in medicine. While it was not possible to interview every retired physician, I did try to include those that represented each specialty or area of practice.

My thanks to Georgia Keeney, Ed.D., for her encouragement, her guidance, and her excellent editing; to James L. Anderson, M.D., and Donald K. Haynes, Ph.D., for their review and helpful comments; and to Herb Dillon for his help with the photography. And to all of the physicans who participated in this project—for your enthusiasm, your forthrightness, and your willingness to pass along what you have learned—thank you.

Kathleen Hannan
October, 1996

I can't recall when I decided to become a doctor, but it was very early. Our family practitioner influenced me; I remember him coming to our home often.

The war broke out while I was at St. Olaf and they switched to a three-year curriculum, six days a week. Just turned the crank and spit us out. I was practicing medicine at twenty-three.

After the army, obstetrics seemed very attractive to me. Even as an intern, hospitals treated you like a physician, put you in a position of decision making beyond what the other services did. I asked St. Mary's if I could take a pathology residency—I'd done pathology work as a resident—just until the OB residency started. By fall I realized what I wanted, and I stayed.

Pathologists were a drag on the budget in 1953. We generated no significant income, and yet we had to be paid. Positions for pathologists were scarce. I wrote all over the place with the goal of finding the smallest place that would have me but which also had a first-rate medical staff.

The case I remember most was a four-year-old boy with leukemia. A local physician had a hematologist friend from out east stop for a visit. He said that they had experimented with a dramatic concept—bone marrow transplant—and was optimistic that it might work in the future. Next morning we had a meeting, and the physician told me what he had done. We did the fourth bone marrow transplant in the country at that time and we got a temporary take. I can't believe we did, we did it so crudely at that time. I remember the drama of trying to work out the details because there weren't many precedents.

Most dramatic advance? That's easy. It is the ability to control the sequence of events of a disease. When I began, we tried to diagnose, then prognosticate, and the rest was reassurance and symptomatic relief. The ability to control the course of events now is just incredible.

My interest in the Arctic was just my identity crisis. When we prepare ourselves for a field and first finish our training, we can hardly wait for breakfast to end so we can get at it. That spark and tingle of the new is just exhilarating. But after a certain interval you begin to evolve algorithms, until fifteen years after you start you have algorithms for 95 percent of things that walk in the door. You begin to say, what else is there? I felt I had to do something tangible. I thought that what was preventing me from recognizing the truth about things was the layers of rationalization that we plaster on our basic motives to make them more acceptable. I thought if I could live with people that were living so close to the edge of survival that they couldn't afford to hide their motives, I was much more apt to understand my own. I contacted the Hudson Bay Company, and we found a family that was willing to put up with me. I did whatever they did, lived on their terms. During subsequent trips to various parts of the arctic, I realized that I had stumbled onto the last group of Eskimos still living in the field and there was no study of these people after one hundred years of contact with the white man. I took a young man named Jim Brandenburg with me, and we did a documentary motion picture that today resides in Canada's National Heritage museum.

It is an incredible privilege to spend your life in this way. It is true that we probably lived during the golden age, but still, if you have a biological bent, it is the ultimate experience.

~

 ℞ *Be aware of the incredible degree to which you can enrich your lives if you are willing to earn 20 percent less than the most you possibly could. A medical career is going to provide you a comfortable life. Squeezing every drop out beyond that is not necessary. If you're willing to earn a little less and take the difference in time and use that time for other interests, it is unbelievable how much richer you can make your life's experiences.*

4

CHARLES M. BAGLEY, M.D.
GENERAL SURGERY

I was born in Palent, Oregon, on a fruit ranch up in the foothills. I lived there until I was five and we moved back to Duluth. I've been here since 1915; it's been our home. I went to Stanford Medical School, interned in St. Paul, and then in 1938 came back and went into practice with my father and my sister Elizabeth.

Elizabeth had been here since 1927. We had an office in the Medical Arts Building; office calls were $3 or $4. We did a lot of surgery for a very nominal fee and made house calls. Complete obstetric care was $35.00. The nurse anesthetist was usually trained by the physician who was doing the surgery. It was either chloroform or ether: we kept giving it until they slowed their breathing; we tried to keep them even. Intubation was very modern. The relaxant drugs, curare and so forth were most helpful. Otherwise, everyone was struggling to keep the patient from straining—yelling at the anesthetist to get them down more.

Sulfas were just coming in, quite magic for awhile. Penicillin not until 1941 or 42, even then very limited. I was in the navy in 1942, and in the Azores. When we came into town, the people said "The head of Standard Oil here has a huge infection in his arm that nobody can cure, he's very sick. Can you see him?" I said, "Sure." I injected the whole area with novocain and penicillin. In two days he was well. It was really the magic bullet then.

One day, I was called up on the Central Hillside to see a boy who was having stomach pains. He was eleven years old, and it was obvious he had a ruptured appendix. The father was born in the old country, Eastern Europe, and he said "No, I'm not taking him to the hospital, it's too expensive. He's not worth it." So between my father and myself, we practically kidnapped that boy and took him to St. Mary's and drained his abscess, but he was still terribly sick. That was before penicillin. We gave him as much sulfa as we dared, in a number of small transfusions, and eventually it cleared up. About five years ago, I was up on St. Marie Street, and a fellow stopped and said "You don't remember me, do you?" I said, "I can't remember your last name, your first name is Johnny. When you were eleven, you had a ruptured appendix." He couldn't believe it.

In the prepenicillin days, I remember cases of pneumonia that should have gotten well if we'd had something to treat them with. We had nothing except rest, oxygen, and hope. I can remember quite a number of young people we lost that we shouldn't have, we wouldn't have five or six years later.

We tried to give the best care we could. Some things were beyond our care—brain problems, pancreatic problems were pretty obscure until they got to be very serious. With orthopedic things, it's much more helpful to have something besides just X rays to see what's going on. A lot of it you had to do by experience or intuition. My father and sister had been in practice much longer than I. They could come up with a diagnosis that I'd been struggling with for three or four days. They'd say, well that's simple, it's this or that. You gradually developed a sense about things.

Three of our children became doctors. We never told any of them what to do, they made their own choice.

We were driving back from our place up north in 1980, talking about government encroachment and taxes, and I decided I'll just quit. So I put a notice in the paper and quit two weeks later. It wasn't hard. I missed the clinical part but I didn't miss those insurance forms.

Next time I'd take a cue from my kids and take more time off. All of us were on call all the time. We had Saturday office hours. It was tough for quite a number of years.

℞ *Listen to your patient. A number of people who are in practice now trained in large, municipal hospitals. They didn't have time to sit down and talk to everybody and they kind of got out of the habit. I know our local medical school is very strongly clued in to the patient rather than to what you think their problem might be.*

8

My family was very involved in medicine. My brother and my father were both physicians. I had no children; I was never married, so I had to keep track of the whole bunch. Someone in the family got a little bag and put in various things they thought would represent what a doctor's bag should have. Everybody took it for granted that I would need this bag, but I can't remember ever being asked if I wanted the bag.

I went to Carleton College and then to medical school at the University of Michigan, graduated in 1927. I stayed on at Michigan for another three years, and when I came home to Duluth in 1930, I went into my father's practice—he did considerable surgery, and surgery was my specialty. There was an awful lot of work being done, but very little evidence of change.

I hadn't even thought about it until somebody asked me recently, but I practiced for almost exactly fifty years. It just seems as if it went along from day to day. Some days were a lot of work.

We were doing as much of the early work as we could, and yet we weren't accomplishing any wonders. This group of doctors was very harmonious, noted for their ability to get along with one another. I went to a meeting regarding some of the early work on outpatient teaching; within a year or so, we began to see more results with outpatient work, and in the next ten years we made a lot of improvements. There are so many now, it's hard to keep up.

Even though anesthesia seems ordinary now, it is amazing how much it has changed. In the beginning, we gave our own anesthesia—ether, which is very hazardous, and chloroform, which if used correctly, was very good. What we have now is very skillfully used, carefully prescribed. With that under control, particularly with thoracic surgery, people began to survive that which they could not have survived before. All of a sudden everything was being studied, simple things like fluid balance. It's surprising we got through it at all, it was just very early, very hard work we were doing.

At the beginning of the war you couldn't get penicillin, they were saving it all for the soldiers. I had a case of osteomyelitis, a woman who had bouts ever since she was three, and she was now twenty. We'd get her cleared, and she'd have a recurrence. It was a couple of years before we were able to get some penicillin. I gave her an injection in the knee cavity and it was remarkable the way it cleared up. We used to take care of everything, including neurosurgery. If it was a depressed fracture, you'd try to clean things up as much as you could, then give them penicillin in all manner of ways. We kept the sickest patients in the hospital for weeks at a time. Some I did surgery on now would be out of the hospital in two or three days.

House calls? Oh heavens, yes! I wondered afterwards how we ever did it. From 8 A.M. to 1 P.M. I made calls, and you'd carry the latest samples with you—that's where most of them got tried out. It might be dressings, fresh post-ops. There were so many of those.

It was hard to retire. I think I didn't realize how dependent I was on work. It eases up on you. I just didn't think about living to be over ninety, I was surprised when it happened. I must have been easy to work with.

I like people. I'm sure I'm not the smartest person who came along, but you do the best you can. I like people, and I think the patient comes first.

~

 R℞ *I can't think of anything else I would do. I didn't consider my patients any trouble at all. If you've been caring for a family for many years, you can almost tell on the phone what's wrong with them. When medicine gets to be business, you get away from the homey feeling that patients yearn for. But they can't get it back because doctors didn't make any money in those days.*

12

JOHN D. BARKER, M.D.
FAMILY MEDICINE

I interned at St. Mary's in 1939. That first year I went out to a little town called Warren in the Red River Valley. I'd never been up in that area before. The first night I was driving toward town I saw a car coming and dimmed my lights. It was five minutes before that car actually came.

I was in the service for five years. I entered during peacetime, went in for a year, but the Japanese extended that a little bit. I was a flight surgeon in England. When I came back to Duluth, I didn't know what I would do. I went up to Ely to help Dr. Grahek for a time, but I was living in a hotel and my wife and child were in St. Paul. It was costing me more than I was making. Meanwhile, Dr. Ryan, our old family doctor in Morgan Park, asked if I would help him out for a few weeks—his mother had just died. And I stayed from 1946–70. From 1970–75, I ran the occupational health service at St. Luke's. I retired from there, and we went down to Florida for a year. But I started feeling punk, and when you're sick, there's no place like home and no doctors like your own. So I came back.

When Dr. Ryan died, Dr. Franklin Johnson came. It worked out well; Morgan Park was a good place to practice. My office was across the street from the high school, and I knew everybody. I took my car to work every day because I made a lot of house calls. It was nice to have the car and bag sitting right out in front. And I'd go over to the cement plant for an hour every day, five days a week. We didn't take appointments. They just showed

13

up, and I stayed until they were gone. Some of them would call and say "Well, how many are in the waiting room?" Those who complained about no appointments are the people who also complain about waiting at the Duluth Clinic for an appointment. I guess you just can't win.

I especially remember one case. There used to be a veteran's project in Morgan Park, and in it lived a family that had a child every February. Home deliveries. I remember the first time I went, there were some neighbors there. One gal said she would give her the ether or chloroform; one said she'd help me; and the other said she'd take care of the baby. Well, the baby started coming and all three of them passed out. The only ones awake were the patient and I.

At the plant, the burns were the worst. They were horrible because they were so painful to begin with, before you could give anything for relief of pain. We had excellent nurses, and the guys from the garage would drive the ambulance. We also had amputations—that was hard. But the plant was pretty good about taking care of the men, giving them some kind of a job after they healed.

Of course, there's the discovery of penicillin. And the specialization of the hospitals was a big change, they have sections for everything. And the nurses are better trained. They were a great help because you felt that a patient was in good hands when you left. And the emergency room improved. Technology has been an improvement, especially in analgesia.

I don't know if I'd do it again. I've thought about that. I probably wouldn't go into general practice. I think now I might specialize. I don't know what I'd specialize in because I enjoyed general practice, but there's no question your life would be easier. Although I never thought I'd live this long, my life must have agreed with me. I think you enjoy it more because you realize the things you get, you've earned. I can't complain. I did very well.

~

 R̶x *Patients are smarter than they used to be. They expect the best of care, they're well read. They know when you're sloughing them off. I don't think they expect too much, but the ones who expect the most never pay. Your office expenses are the same for one as for two.*

16

ROBERT O. BERGAN, M.D.
PEDIATRICS

I was born in a little Norwegian/Swedish community in western Minnesota named Clinton. People used to ask me how to spell it. They don't anymore. My dad was a country doctor and a general surgeon who took care of five little communities. My mother was a nurse anesthetist for the whole county, which in those days was unusual; she was a pioneer. My dad used to say his only claim to fame was that he was his wife's husband. She was on the go all the time. It was just me and my brother, who is also a doctor. So the neighbors brought us up; little towns are that way.

I missed a lot of school when I was a kid. Dad would come and take me out of school to scrub in on farm accidents, so I could tie the knots and steady the retractors. My mother would administer the anesthesia, Dad would do the repair work, and I'd be first assistant.

My brother and I joked about it because we didn't know there was any other way to make a living. That's all Mother and Dad ever talked about, medical things. This was in the day of home deliveries; when I was in high school, I delivered several babies. There weren't any trained midwives so they trained me. I would go one place to deliver a baby and my mom would go another, and my dad a third. It was crazy.

I always wanted to go into pediatrics. My wife and I both wanted to live in Duluth. We spent our honeymoon here along the North Shore, and we decided this was where we wanted to live. We came in September of 1947, and we've been here ever since.

Roe and Nutting and I started in the old clinic on Second Street. We expanded as much as we could, but there was no more space. We saw an awful lot of patients in the old days. We'd make rounds at seven or eight o'clock in the morning and start office appointments at ten. We'd go all day until six o'clock, and then we'd go back to the hospital. When the polio vaccine first came in, everybody came and registered whether I saw them or not. One day I had two hundred thirty registrations. I didn't see them all, but I saw a lot.

In the days when my dad was practicing, there weren't any antibiotics, no specific drugs for anything. There was just surgery and people got well by themselves. The best he had was sulfa. But I had a little vial of penicillin. We'd give a kid with osteomyelitis 3,000 units every three hours, and it was the most dramatic thing how these kids would get well.

Yes, I think I would go into medicine again. My son's a doctor, he's doing very well, but he doesn't enjoy practicing medicine like I did, not at all. I used to have fun in my practice. Little girls would give a kiss, and little boys a hug. Aren't allowed to do that now, it would be sexual harassment. And I had nicknames for them all, can't do that anymore. I suppose I'd do it again, but I wouldn't enjoy it.

There were a lot of strange cases. I remember one, nasty in a sense. A little girl came over from Michigan; she had a good, conscientious doctor who had treated her for vaginal discharge for a long time. He did a culture and thought it looked like gonococcus. Well, a sweet little five-year-old isn't going to get gonorrhea. The odor was foul, just awful. So I had the nurse help me, and we used a tiny speculum and found a bobby pin that had been up in her vagina for months. I don't know why it didn't perforate, the abscess was awful. It cleared right up.

~

R̲x̲ *Where we really need physicians is out in small communities. But with all the changes in health care, many small hospitals are closing. We need family practitioners, it's really very necessary. You can train young doctors, but if they don't have hospitals, they can't do anything.*

I was an only child, born in Mason City, Iowa, in 1907. Hard to tell when I decided to become a doctor. My father was an educated farmer, my mother a school teacher. Her father emigrated from Denmark, drove horses for the country doctor, became a pharmacist, and then a physician. I suppose that progression was influential. Although my parents did not try to direct me, they were anxious for me to go to college. I got a scholarship to Grinnell College, then transferred to the University of Iowa.

When I was in high school, I developed severe hay fever. My dad said, "Why don't you talk to the insurance man, he drives to Duluth for his hay fever every fall?" So I drove up here when I was fifteen or sixteen, and when I came over the hill my hay fever disappeared miraculously. I always remembered that. When I finished medical school, I was in the army, and when it came to internships, I elected to come up here. There were two very good internships at St. Luke's and St. Mary's. They were competitive and had an excellent reputation throughout the Midwest. My dean called St. Luke's and said "I've got a nice young man who wants to come up there, and I think you should take him." They said, "Okay." It was that simple in those days.

We got married when my wife graduated, the year before I did. She taught school for a year; we have never been as wealthy since. When we interned, my widowed aunt who always liked Duluth said she'd drive us. So we packed a couple of suitcases and a box of books, and that's how we got here.

I went into private practice in a little building at the end of the Woodland car line. At the same time, UMD was looking for a director of student health, so I did both until I got called into the air force and was sent to the Azores from 1951–53. I returned for a few years, but in 1957, I decided it was finally time for me to do what I had wanted to do, which was surgery, and after my first year, my good friends Drs. Fifield and Streitz influenced me toward urology. I'm forever thankful because it worked out to be a very good relationship.

It's difficult to pin down one advancement, one development leads to another. Renal dialysis was a big development; it in turn led to renal transplantation, and that expanded to involve other organ systems. Fiberoptics made a big jump forward in endoscopic surgery. The improvement of lighting was a big breakthrough, so was open urologic surgery. And now stone disease is managed with lithotripsy, and almost entirely without open surgery. I've discussed and written about a variety of unusual cases; wouldn't pick any single one. You like to remember those that turned out well; I guess I've had more victories than defeats.

I have five wonderful kids, but none of them are in medicine. I can't think of a more rewarding life. Where else can you do so much good stuff for people? No place. Medicine and nursing are the highest professions the Almighty has created. I really feel that. And education gets in there, too.

Retirement was a hard adjustment. I suppose if you were more methodical, you'd be better prepared. There are adjustments that take time, and I don't think there is any shortcut. I didn't have a single hobby, but I enjoyed a lot of different things, and I still do.

My patients liked me and I liked them; if we didn't have a good relationship, I moved them because getting well is a team effort. You make a judgement, you suggest, and you set off on a course of treatment. In the present system, communications are lost to some degree. I don't like being a health care provider, I like being a doctor. And I don't like my patient being a client, I like my patient to be a patient.

℞ *Listen to your patients. Avoid intellectual arrogance, which I think is the worst sin of physicians. Once that comes across, your patient resents you. Don't be afraid to work to an end rather than to a time. Don't stop because your eight hours is up or you're heading into your vacation. And it's critical to continue your education regularly and in depth. If you fail to do so, you will be out of the system. Things have changed so rapidly, if you do not attend meetings, do not do your reading, do not think about the things you're treating in an innovative way, you'll lose it. I used to liken it to shoveling coal. The faster you shovel, the faster it falls in on you. To shovel successfully, you work hard.*

24

I was born in Chicago. My father was an OB/GYN specialist in the navy. That was unusual. He died without ever seeing me become a physician.

I was a navy brat. We spent one year in Shanghai, China, and I graduated from the American high school there. After my junior year in college, I joined the RCAF as a Signal Corps cadet and was there two-and-a-half years. I can't tell you why I decided to become a doctor; although I remember making the decision while I was in France. I went to Dartmouth College for two years and then two years at Harvard. I interned at Magill University in Toronto and did a three-year residency at the University of Minnesota, specializing in pulmonary disease.

I was at Northwestern University for one year as an instructor of medicine, then I came back to the University of Minnesota as an instructor for two years, and then I came to Duluth. I had been up the North Shore, and I liked the area. The clinic offered me a job, and I said I'd take it. It was very simple. That was 1956, and I retired in 1987.

I saw patients at all three hospitals, until seven or eight o'clock at night. I made a lot of house calls. I saw fifteen patients a day; a good workup took a long time to do so I worked a lot of hours. We used to take call every six weeks, we spent a lot of time at the hospitals covering for the weekends. We really worked hard in those days. I think there were twenty-eight physicians in the clinic when I started and one hundred fifty when I left.

They had a good clerical staff; it was a very good organization. Duluth has excellent medical care.

Retirement was no problem at all. I manage to stay very busy on the computer, with Rotary, and church. I've been active all along. I canoed for twenty years and sailed for thirteen. We have a lake place and do a lot of traveling. We have seven children but none became physicians.

Sure, I would do it again. It's been a very good decision for me. I've enjoyed it thoroughly. It was very worthwhile.

The greatest advance to me was in antituberculin chemotherapy. I treated lung disease medically, using streptomycin, INH, and PAS. Those drugs made a big difference to my patients, making it possible for them to be treated on an outpatient basis. It doesn't surprise me that TB is coming back. More resistant bugs are emerging, and it's a real problem.

We gave excellent medical care at the time, really good. But it's better now, in the sense that you can do more. Medicine has changed a lot in Duluth. The specialties have compartmentalized medicine; it's hard to find a doctor that covers everything, and that compartmentalizes care. But it's interesting, there is still continuity. And you don't have to worry about their skills.

Occasionally cases are really altered by using a CT or MRI, but you can't do them on everybody. We did a lot of X rays, and there was a lot of cost there, too. You have to be selective about their use. I suspect national health care is in our future, and I'm all for it. I'm in the minority I know, but I've been in the minority about a lot of things since I came here.

R_X *Pay attention to the work you do. Be honest and caring. Don't care too much about your earning capacity. I don't think young people work like we did; they won't put in the hours. They have more free time, are more self-oriented. We worked too hard in our day, probably. There should be a happy medium someplace.*

28

ROBERT J. CAMPAIGNE, M.D.
FAMILY MEDICINE

Oh yes, yes, I was born in Duluth. Arnold Swenson delivered me. My sister and I were home deliveries. I cost $50, and I think my sister cost $35. She's three years older so she was cheaper. Everybody was a home delivery. Even had your tonsils removed in the office. Like another era, wasn't it?

My dad was a machinist on the railroad, and then he taught school. I got all his tools; I've got quite a machine shop. I always tell everybody I got half his talent and all his tools, and that seems to be enough. I worked at St. Luke's, the youngest orderly they hired. And we got $.75 an hour. But UMD was only $50 a quarter and medical school was $129 a quarter, so we were very lucky—the last of the kids to really get in on the ground floor. We must be rich doctors.

I went to medical school at Minnesota, 1954–58. Then I worked with Arnold Swenson for four years in West Duluth; we were above the old Gopher Cafe. We moved to the new building, and I worked until 1962. We were there every day working, that's how you got all the clientele. And they stay with you forever, you know. I went back for my surgery residency at the university and finished that in 1969. That seems so long ago, 1969. Then I came back to work with Arnold, and he retired in 1970. He was the same age as the year. Now they're all gone.

I went out to Morgan Park with Frank Johnson. He left in 1982, and I closed up shop in October of '89. I was alone for about six years. That's hard. I was up at 5 A.M., back in the office after supper, dictating and calling people on their reports. My first wife died after childbirth and left me with a two-week-old kid. I can still change diapers in the dark if I have to. I fed him in the morning; I would run to the hospital and run to the office and then be home at noon, feed him again, run back to the office, be back home by five; and in the evening I'd take him for a ride. For two or three solid years I did that, and those were busy times, busy times. I took him with me all the time. It was very busy. You can't maintain that schedule, but I did it a long time. I had a couple of TIAs, and then I had the real good-sized stroke in June 1990, about six months after I quit. I'm surviving.

The case I remember most was the third case I ever saw, a child with meningococcal meningitis. A woman came in carrying this little girl, said she'd had a little sore throat for about a day. By the time she'd brought her in she had petechial hemorrhages through her body and a 105 degree temp. I said, "Honey, we got to get her to the hospital in a hurry." I had a brand new Renault then, and I drove her to St. Luke's. This was before the fancy highway, right down Superior Street. The first thing we did was put in lines and give her sulfadiazine, penicillin, and chloramphenicol, and pretty soon the red spots were gone. And that was the sickest kid I think I ever had.

I think transplants and open heart surgery have been the most important developments. I gave quite a bit to the program here because I think it was so important, and we worked hard to get it.

You know, no one's clairvoyant. How do you know what you would have done if you've never done it? But I would never do it again. It's too hard, much too hard. When I started, malpractice insurance was less than $500 a year. When I finished it was $24,000. No. I would go into engineering if I were to do it again.

~

 ℞ *Everything's working against the lone practitioner nowadays, no matter what they tell you. The system is geared for a massive group practice, excluding the primary physician. No matter what they tell you, you can't survive. I think it was fun. And now it's dying, if it's not already dead, and just not buried. When I first started it was 90 percent fun and 10 percent problems. When I finished it was 90 percent problems and 10 percent fun. And that's not an acceptable ratio at all.*

CLARENCE H. CHRISTENSEN, M.D.
FAMILY MEDICINE

My father was a Danish immigrant to this country, a blacksmith. My mother and her parents came from Norway and Sweden. I was born in Iowa in 1912, the oldest of three children. I spoke Danish until I was five; then my mother died after pelvic surgery and all the housekeepers spoke English, so all the Danish went out the door.

When I graduated from high school, I started pre-engineering at Morningside College. A dentist came to town. He had no money, so he came to my dad's shop, and my dad made him some dental tools. I would sit down and look at his books, and I took some home and started talking to him, and he said, "Why don't you go into medicine?" I went to the University and talked to the dean, and he was so great—he figured out what courses I would need, and I went into medical school at Iowa university that fall, 1936. When I interned, the dean said, "I have two positions in Duluth right now, you won't have to apply somewhere and wait for an answer." So I came. My wife was the supervisor in pediatrics at St. Luke's and that's where I met her.

I worked for the summer in Biwabik for two doctors there who wanted somebody to relieve them so they could take a vacation; they hadn't had one in a long time. While I was there, Dr. Karl Johnson called and asked me to come to Duluth because he had to go into the navy. So I came down and worked in the West End; the war was starting then; we were all just biding our time. And then I was in the navy for four years, 1942–46. I had known Dr. Rudie when I was in Duluth, and I met him again in the navy. He was out before me, and he wrote and asked if I would come and practice with him. Two of us to start with, and then Dr. Grohs came, and then Dr. Rudie's son, Bill, and then Dr. Blum. It was such a compatible group; it was great to have that sort of relationship, just a hand shake and your word. We were flexible with call time, a really good arrangement. I started in 1946 and retired in 1985.

You remember the horrible things. One pregnant woman had an acute appendicitis—it was gangrenous. Everything went fine until the placenta came out, and then she went into gram negative shock, and even with antibiotics she died the next day. And here's the father and the live baby and the other children. And then I had a lady who'd just delivered, and the nurses went back to check her—everything was fine. The next time they came in she was dead, a ruptured cerebral aneurysm. And there was another father with children. Both times it reminded me of my dad, the connections between them.

My cat had a tooth pulled recently, and it cost more then the deliveries I used to do. We charged $45 in '46, and if the baby was a boy, the circumcision was free. We took care of the baby, too. It was a bargain.

The biggest difference? Oh, the penicillin. In the South Pacific, we had three wounded marines and before we could get to them, they had gas gangrene. The first two came in, and they died. The last one came, and they had this penicillin they'd never used, so they used it on him, and he came out of it great—it was just amazing. It was wonderful.

We have six children; one of my sons is a physician in the emergency room in Hayward. They saw me as busy, but I was out a lot during the night. I always tried to get home for meals. I'd save house calls for after I helped put the kids to bed, so I could see them every night.

Retirement is great. It's like a vacation that just keeps going on and on. We ski, bicycle, do a lot of walking.

~

 Rₗ *Do what you like to do. Live in the area that you would like to live. Enjoy your time off. I like the more simple life, down to earth. In a smaller town you have so many friends, real genuine friends.*

36

GEORGE M. COWAN, M.D.
PSYCHIATRY

I was born in Oakland California, I'm one of the older ones. My father was a working man; I was the first doctor in the family; seven others have followed since. In high school I decided to become a doctor, don't know why, I just decided. My last four years were at Minnesota, and I graduated in 1936. I interned at St. Mary's from 1936 to July '37. Times were tough then, so I took a job with the CCC in Brimson for two years. Bored to death. I answered a Veteran's Administration ad looking for doctors in psychiatry, which I was interested in. I was accepted, but after two years I went overseas, took sick in Germany, and was sent home on sick leave. Didn't know what I was going to do. I applied for a psychiatry residency at the University and was accepted. I took my boards in May 1948 and was made assistant chief of psychiatry at the Veteran's Hospital. My wife was a Duluth girl and wanted to come here, so I found an office in the Medical Arts Building for $59 a month; that was February 1954, and I practiced until June 1, 1989. That last office cost $1,000 a month. I was alone until 1968, and then my son joined me. I practiced psychiatry for two months shy of fifty years. That's a long time. Too long.

The advent of medications is probably the most dramatic advance in psychiatry. In about 1949, Thorazine came out, the first drug of psychiatry. What a tremendous advance. Of course, the other change is the number of psychologists. When I came to town, there was one; now you open the

phone book, there are hundreds. Teachers, preachers, everybody's a thera-
pist. All the talk shows on TV are doing therapy. Good or bad, it made a
difference.

When I first practiced, I charged $15 an hour for six or seven patients
a day, and we didn't get paid in all those cases. Charging is one thing, collecting is another. If somebody would call and ask me to see someone in a
hurry, I'd say sure, send them in. I'd squeeze them in someplace. It's important; as long as I had the time, why should I turn them away? And there
were lots of frustrating moments. They'd call in the middle of the night, at
two o'clock in the morning, to tell you they couldn't sleep. "I didn't wake
you, did I doctor?" I'd say, "Hell no, I had to get up to answer the phone." I
made five or six thousand dollars in 1954, enough to get by on. A dollar
was worth something then, I bought a new Chevrolet for $1,200. Times
have changed.

I don't know if I'd do it again. That's a hard question to answer. I
can't do it again, so how would I know what I'd do?

There's one case I've always thought of. A girl put her two little babies
in a sack and threw them into Lake Michigan. Of course, she was not con-
victed by reason of insanity. But she was schizophrenic, really very sick.
When I came to Kankakee, she had recently been admitted with a twenty-
four hour guard. She showed absolutely no progress at all. I took over her
treatment, dismissed the guards, and right away she started getting better—
so well that after she was discharged, she got herself a job, a good job, too,

and ultimately got married. That's one I've always recalled. Most of the cases I think about were the criminal cases, they stick in your mind.

Retirement wasn't difficult at all. The practice was getting to be a pain in the you-know-what. I retired when I was seventy-nine, which is too old really. I could be busier but I have trouble getting around—bad legs and feet. I'm active in the Boy's and Girl's Clubs and the Lions, we have lots of friends. My wife and I play gin rummy once a day. For money—otherwise it's no fun. It hasn't been dull. I sleep late, if I have to get up early it kills me.

∼

 R̥ *I liked what I did very much. Be honest with yourself and with your patients. Don't expect to go into practice by yourself, like they used to. Stay with a group in the rural areas, four, five, or six people.*

ROBERT J. DEUTSCH, M.D.
FAMILY MEDICINE, EMERGENCY ROOM

I always wanted to be a doctor. My brother went to dental school, and I went to medical school at Marquette University in Milwaukee. That's where I met my wife, Peg. I interned at St. Mary's—I was born here in the old east wing— and then went into the air force for two years. I returned to Duluth and started my practice in 1957. I joined the Spang Clinic in the West End, and we practiced there until 1976. When the others retired, I went into emergency medicine at St. Mary's and retired in December 1987. I have seven children so far.

The most unusual cases are usually the most frightening. An aunt called me at ten o'clock and said her sister's baby had a cough and wasn't acting right. I said, "Bring her right down." I saw that little baby at noon. She was ashen gray, had one little red spot on the cheek, and one on the chest. I called the intern and said, "Do a spinal tap and blood cultures and call me right away." The intern called me when she got there and said the baby had generalized purpura. I said, "Forget the spinal tap, get a blood culture, start the baby on penicillin and sulfa." That baby was dead by two o'clock in the afternoon. Now that's a frightening thing, a three-month-old baby dead in a period of four hours. You have no control over it. That was a case I'll remember for a long time.

The most dramatic changes I've seen are in antibiotics and chemo-therapy. That's what made people live a lot longer. When I was in the service, a young airman came in. His record said that he had been in several times before for headaches, so I put him in the hospital and did a spinal tap. He had TB meningitis. I put him on methambutal and streptomycin at the same time, and he recovered. Before that time it was 100 percent fatal. In 1918, when you got pneumonia, 50 percent of people died, and the ones that lived were out of work for six months to a year. That was a great thing, penicillin. Most people don't realize what antibiotics have done and what had gone on before that.

St. Mary's got a CAT scan two weeks before I saw a lady who came to the emergency room complaining of headaches. Something bothered me about how she said it. I found out she was a heavy smoker and sent her for a chest X ray. She had a large mass. She said that she had worked with kids for years but now they were starting to bother her. I thought she might have a frontal lobe tumor, so I sent her for a CAT scan. She had multiple tumors in her head. In less than two hours we knew she had a serious illness and knew what it was. I was very impressed. It saved her a lot of invasive tests and a long hospitalization.

I saw about twenty patients a day. We tried to limit the number of people so we could take time to talk to them. That's one of the major complaints that a lot of people had; their doctor didn't explain things to them. So we spent time and talked to our patients.

Medicine has been good to me. I hope I've been good to it, but it's been good to me. We are retired now and both like it down in Nevada. One of the real negatives I'm noticing as I get older is the lack of sunlight in Duluth. I don't mind the snow or the cold, but I hate those endless gray days. Down there, it's a sunny day every single day. We really enjoy it.

∾

 R̽ *Medicine is very rewarding, but there are certain requirements of medicine now that make it almost impossible, in my opinion, for a young doctor to go into a small community alone. I think it's wonderful that they want to go into a small town and they're certainly needed and appreciated. But unless you have some physician close by or with you, I think it's an impossible task. It takes a special individual, because you're isolated, you have to do it on your own, you can't depend on anyone else. It's just too hard. And it's hard on your family, too.*

44

I am an only child, born in International Falls. My father was an auto mechanic and worked in the garage for what was then the Minnesota-Ontario Paper Company, now Boise Cascade. My mother was a housewife.

I don't know as I really ever did decide to become a doctor. I think I went into it at the urging of my mother; if left to my own devices, I probably would have ended up in the paper mill. But after I graduated from high school, she talked me into going into premed, which I did for three years at Loyola University in Chicago, and then I went into med school.

My ENT residency was kind of fate, too. I started out in general surgery at the Mayo Clinic. My first elective was ENT. I liked it, and they were looking for residents in the field at that time. I finished in September 1959, and then in January 1960, I went into the air force and was fortunate enough to be based in Spain. I spent two-and-a-half years doing ENT there, a wonderful experience. My wife was a dental technician at the base clinic, and we were married before I left Spain. Coming to Duluth was a real culture shock, but she adapted very well.

Before I left for the air force, I made a commitment to the Duluth Clinic. I had visited here and talked to Joe Leek, who was the only otolaryngologist in the clinic at that time. I agreed that I would come back when I finished my tour of duty, and I started at the clinic on the first of October 1962. Dr. Leek and I were the only two for quite a number of years, and we were very busy, on call every weekend and every night for fifteen years until Dr. Portilla came. Toward the end, we did reach an agreement with Bill Merrick and Jim Anderson, who at that time were at the Medical Arts Building, and we alternated weekend call with them. That took a lot of pressure off.

I had a lot of difficult cases, a lot I'd like to forget. I enjoyed doing surgery—ear and cancer. That was probably the most enjoyable part of the practice, but of course working in the office could be interesting, too.

There have been so many advances in medical technology—CT scans, MRIs, the increase in the effective use of antibiotics. The biggest change would have to be the encroachment by the government and the insurance companies on the practice of medicine. Changed it completely. That is, to me, very disheartening, to have either an agent of the federal government or the state of Minnesota or an insurance company dictate how to practice medicine. Medicine is, you might say, going down the tubes. The relationship between physician and hospital and between physician and patient has changed. It is more of an adversarial relationship now.

Medical costs, at least in this area, haven't gone up that much if you compare them to the cost of a stamp or a new car. A stamp has gone up ten times and a car used to cost three or four thousand dollars. So I think it's too bad that physicians didn't have a better organized campaign against the takeover of medicine by government and insurance companies.

I'm not really done, I'm semiretired. I have a plane, so I fly outreach for the Clinic— to the Falls twice a month and to Ely once. You have to go on, you can't just sit and vegetate.

I have two children, neither of whom was interested in medicine. My son, Peter, is an airline pilot, and my daughter, Victoria, is working with my wife in her gourmet coffee stores, España and the Blue Note Cafe.

~

 R℞ *Treat the patient like you would want to be treated. Work hard and keep your nose clean. And yes, I think I would do it again. I think my colleagues and I knew medical practice in the good days. We were fortunate to be able to practice when we did because it has all changed now.*

48

I don't really know when I decided to be a doctor. I started at the University of Minnesota School of Engineering, I thought about geology or petroleum engineering. But after my first year, I knew I wanted to do something else. There was an OB/GYN resident I had a chat with, and I told him I had the idea I would rather be a physician. I had never given that a great deal of thought prior to that time. He said, "Well, if you have this idea in your mind, you have to give it a shot. If you don't, you'll never be satisfied." So with those words of wisdom, I changed my major and went into premed. I suppose it was fate. My schooling was interrupted by the service—I ended up as a marine fighter pilot—then graduated from medical school in 1950. I interned in the navy and then did a urology fellowship in Minneapolis. I came to Duluth in 1954 and have been here ever since.

I came to Duluth because I had hay fever, and this was reportedly the hay fever relief capital of the world. That proved to be not quite true, but all the time I was here I got along well. I practiced by myself for the first year, then Dr. Streitz joined me and we practiced together for thirty-four years. We'd been in practice awhile when Dr. Brooker joined us and then years later Dr. Hutchens.

I've never been unhappy about choosing urology. It's been a wonderful specialty, primarily because, from a surgical perspective, you know exactly what the problem is and how to attack it. There is seldom any time when there is exploratory surgery for urologic problems. You know what it is and how to take care of it. That's a very comforting way of involving yourself in the surgical aspects of a specialty.

There were cases where there were coexisting problems, where you thought you were handling one problem and it turned out there was another one in the same individual. I had one patient I thought had a cyst. He had the cyst, but right behind the cyst he had a malignancy in the kidney. I could easily have made a mistake and just gone ahead and treated the one and overlooked the other.

Urology was an ever-changing scene. We did only one nephrectomy for TB, due to antitubercular drugs. And renal stone surgery practically disappeared with the use of the lithotripter. Cancer remained the problem—prostatic, renal, and bladder. Diagnostics are better, but not always the outcome.

Sure, I'd do it again. Now it isn't like it was when we started, but I'm sure that happens. I'm sure there were guys who had been here in practice when we came who would say you should go away, you should become a plumber. I wouldn't discourage anybody from going into medicine, but I'm just so damn glad I'm out I can hardly stand it.

Retirement is hard. I miss the interplay; we had a fun practice. I knew more about my patients than I did about their illness. I knew what kind of bees they raised, everything. And we seemed to have enough time to do that, we were all that way. That I miss. It's hard to slow your gyro down when you're up early, work all day long, home maybe at eight o'clock. But I didn't cave in, there's always something more for you to do if you have the health to do it. That was that life, now we're on a different life. That is the way it should be. You're out of it, but you can still make some contributions.

❧

 R_x *You're in the most exciting profession in the world. I wouldn't tell you how it was, there isn't any sense in doing that. Under the heel of the government and third party payers, it's still the most exciting thing in the world. You'll be able to earn a good living, you'll be satisfied because you're doing something for somebody. If you weren't there maybe they wouldn't still be living. If you give it your best shot and you don't make it okay, that's it. You can go do whatever. But there isn't anything like being an M.D.*

52

HENRY F. FISKETTI, M.D.
FAMILY MEDICINE

I interned at St. Mary's in 1936. From there I went to the Herding Hospital, down an Third Street, where the IGA was; it sits partly on the foundation of the old county jail. Dr. Coventry came to me one day and said, "Henry, maybe you'd be interested in this. We want to convert that jail into a fifty-bed hospital; we want somebody to run it and live there, and we'll give you a little apartment for minimal rent." I said, "Well, I suppose I could try it," and I wound up running it for a $100 a month plus room and board. That was my first paid job. I saw hundreds of patients, and I did all the tonsils in town. I had the best bunch of nurses I have ever seen in one spot. I was my own boss there. And the money part of it—I don't know how, but it would last me the whole month. I was never really broke. I was there a year: ate there, slept there, the only doctor, on call twenty-four hours. I'd go out in the middle of the night to see a patient, go back to bed, the next day I wouldn't remember being gone.

After the year at Herding, I opened an office in the Medical Arts Building by myself. This was 1938. It cost me peanuts. All you had to have was four or five chairs, a desk, and a couple of magazines. My total office overhead in the Medical Arts Building, which was then a brand new building, was $150 a month counting a receptionist, rent, and garage.

I was always alone. Every year for the first twenty-five years, I thought about a partner, but when I figured it, it always came out the same. Too costly. I worked through it, but I would never do it again. It's too hard. The kids came along, and gee, I don't remember what the kids looked like. Good thing I've got some snapshots.

In 1943, I enlisted in the coast guard. Before I left, I got all my records under five years old and made a deal with Pete Rudie to take care of them. And it worked out fine because, by the time I came back in 1945, I was right next door to Pete and his five or six associates, so it was a good blend, and we could help each other out. The Medical Arts was the only place I ever practiced except when I took over the emergency room at St. Luke's. I spent ten years to the day there.

It wasn't easy to give up my practice. I had talks with myself for a long time. It was hard because you take care of people all your life and then leave them high and dry. But I was going to be sixty years old and had put in forty years, and I thought that was enough. And I didn't have any fringe benefits. I had a little bit of life insurance, but I didn't have anything in particular saved up. I just decided I had done it enough, solo medicine. It was very difficult for me to write that note to my patients.

I've had some cases that were very difficult. There's a lady who lives here in town who should have died. She didn't. We had no penicillin; we had no antibiotics. Very little of anything was any good to her. I gave her over three gallons of blood, a half pint at a time. That was the only thing that was doing any good. She had pelvic inflammation to begin with. She had peritonitis; she had hepatitis; and she had double pneumonia. In the hospital for three-and-a-half months. And she made it.

R_X *I had an idea years ago. What an interesting thing it would be if some eager guy who's young and likes to write would compile a number of cases, interesting ones, hard ones, ones who didn't die that should have, some that died very easily, all unusual, all different. Brief the reader on the history and physical and lab and what the diagnosis turned out to be. What interesting reading that would be. And the medical students could take that book and read it first year. Before they know anything about it. That would be a book medical students would be nuts about. There's a lot of learning value in a book like that. That would be interesting reading, even for practicing physicians.*

56

I was born in Massachusetts. My father was a dentist, and I went to Dartmouth to take the predental course, but it was the same as the premed course, and I realized I was more interested in medicine. My father was very gracious even though he had enlarged his office for me. I got my M.D. from Harvard in 1943 and went into the navy for two years. Then a six-month surgical residency, a one-year residency in pathology, and then to the Mayo Clinic for five years of thoracic surgery. My mother contracted pulmonary tuberculosis when I was six years old, so I went away to school in the fourth grade and spent the rest of my education in boarding school. She died when I was ten. That's why I was interested in thoracic surgery.

Mayo had just started a formal program in thoracic surgery, and part of the training was a six-month residency at Nopeming Sanitorium. That's how I found Duluth. I liked it here, and they needed a surgeon. Nopeming was a very busy place, full, and there was a waiting list. People with positive sputums were unable to get in because they just took the worst cases. Bed rest wasn't great, but it was all they had. Of course, the thing that turned the corner were the antituberculosis drugs. They made thoracic surgery for TB possible. Before that we did collapse therapy, a pneumothorax, various phases of partial collapse of the chest wall, thoracoplasties—terribly disfiguring—trying to collapse cavities and let the lung rest so it would heal. Attempts at resection surgeries in those days were met with disaster.

Two other things were happening at the same time. The county health department had a very aggressive case-finding control program. If patients were recalcitrant, they were committed. And the population was becoming immune. So when Nopeming closed, the clinic needed a general surgeon, and cancer of the lung and esophagus became my major problems.

There's a case I often quote to people, a young woman with Guillain-Barré syndrome. She was in a private room on pediatrics, completely paralyzed, had a tracheostomy and was on a ventilator. One day the vent stopped working, and I just happened to be in the room. I used an ambu bag to keep her alive because someone filling a main oxygen tank had turned the valve off. She developed tremendous crusting, and almost daily I would literally core out her trachea with a straight bronchoscope. Of course, we couldn't ventilate her while I was doing that, so Mrs. Soderstrom would put her finger on her pulse, and when it would start to slow, she'd tell me, and we would put her back on the vent. You wonder how long you're going to keep this up, but we knew she was alive and we had the feeling she knew what was going on. She was a young mother, couldn't move anything but her eyes; she couldn't speak. She was on the ventilator from November to March. She eventually completely recovered. It really moves me still. So you learn not to give up. As you look back, there are a lot of things that didn't work as well. You don't forget those either.

I loved the practice of surgery. I loved medicine, still do. I retired on my sixty-fifth birthday, had a nice celebration, turned in my door card, and walked away. No problem at all. When you're self-driven, the way most of us are, it never goes away. I am continuously behind in all the things I want to do. The days aren't long enough and the weeks go by so quickly.

∽

 R̲x Learn as much as you can about everything. It's far better to be interested in the science of medicine than in the remunerative part of medicine. In our day we didn't come out of medical school with a big debt as they do today, but you practice better medicine if your object is taking care of people rather than making money. You might not be as rich as some are now, but you'll be well compensated for your work.

60

My parents were born in Duluth, and I was too, January 21, 1924. I graduated from Central, took two years of junior college, and then went to the University of Minnesota. I interned at St. Luke's for fifteen months and then spent two years with the air force in the Philipines. I had a three year residency at the VA Hospital in Minneapolis and came to Duluth in 1953.

I worked first with Dr. Dan Wheeler; I made $7,000 my first year. But in 1955, I went solo in the Medical Arts Building.

We were the specialists, the heart and stomach specialists as internists. As subspecialists came in, the ulcer complications went to gastroenterologists, and the heart attacks ended up with cardiologists. Then general internal medicine tended to resemble adult family medicine. While I was solo, I was more comfortable. I didn't realize to what extent my wife worked, raising four kids without me being home much. It was really difficult when I would spend a lot of time after supper on the phone, calling people with lab reports and the like. I never believed in having some clerical person call and say your pap smear showed an abnormality. I wanted to discuss it because I felt that the patient who gets a call or letter may have some questions. Since we're here to treat the people, not to make total convenience for ourselves, life was a little balanced in favor of the patient and against the family. That was one of the joys of retirement, no more phone calls.

My parents were in the fish and freight business. I remember one day when Dr. Charles Mead was taking care of my father for a critical jaw infection, my mother said, "My boy's going to be a doctor." I was about twelve years old. I never thought of an alternative, I only applied to one medical school—seven hundred applicants for one hundred positions, and I got lucky, it just happened.

After my residency, I discussed with my wife where I should practice. I said, "I'd rather be a middle-sized frog in a middle-sized pond than stay in a big city." And so we came back home.

Penicillin was one of the big improvements, but the most amazing advance during my career is the fact that you can transplant an organ from one person to another. There have been so many advances: public health, nutrition, surgery, anesthesia, dialysis, and nuclear medicine—it's just gargantuan.

Here's a case I remember. In earlier years, we didn't know much about parasites in this area; they're mostly tropical. A man was having a great deal of difficulty with diarrhea. We got stool studies; he had giardiasis, and we cured him. It was satisfying because it was a diagnostic coup, but some of the things that were great stuff in those days are fairly routine now. If you made a great diagnosis then it was based on, "Let's see what the surgeon finds."

Paperwork: It does seem now that paperwork takes time away from patients. And the fact that we had to call and ask permission to admit a patient became a real bone of contention. I mean we were thought to be less than honorable. That got to me.

Would I practice again? Sure. I don't know what else I possibly would or could have done. I might do it differently. I think I'd become a subspecialist early in my career. At that time the internist was the center of the consultation drama, the emergency drama, and the adventure was more sharp. It became somewhat more routine. I would do it again the same way, it's just that we had no other choice.

～

R_X *Everything you have done as a student is going to end up at the tip of your pen. That is the most powerful and the most expensive medical instrument that there is. All of the learning, the anatomy, the physiology, the pharmacology ends up coming from your brain to the end of that little pen. You cannot depend on a secretary or a nurse to know exactly what brand or dose or how often to give it. Your orders determine whether the patient's going to get better or not. They must be compulsively precise and legible. Precision in writing orders is essential. And if you have to print, damn it, print. About nurses: This is for young doctors. If there is an experienced nurse when you start out as a resident or an intern and she gives you some advice, take it. An experienced nurse can be an enormous fountain of information.*

64

WILLIAM H. GOODNOW, M.D.
INTERNAL MEDICINE

I had been in the army a couple of years, and while I was in the basic engineering program, they took a third of us and sent us for screening. Apparently they thought there would be a shortage of doctors. I scored well and started medical school in the army in 1945, about when the war ended. By the time I was discharged, I had finished two years of medical school. I'd enjoyed it, and I saw it was an opportunity I didn't have before. I was pretty broke, so I volunteered for the army medical corps, and this helped pay my way. I graduated from the University of Minnesota in 1948 and finished my residency in internal medicine. I knew some of the people at the Duluth Clinic, and so I came up here.

The total clinic size at that time was thirty-five physicians. It was the same group for a good many years. Not just the specialists, that was the whole clinic. Now I go down there and get lost. Just like everything else, it started booming.

I enjoy my retirement. It wasn't too much of an adjustment. I had a sort of gradual retirement because I had cataract surgery and got into trouble with that. Then I had a total hip replacement. I had enough things that were disruptive that I didn't think I wanted to have to practice anymore. It's terribly easy to be busy. When I was first retired, I was still able to play golf, ski, and mow the lawn. I guess I'm kind of lazy at heart. It's quite a change if you're busy at work all day long.

I don't know whether it's a blessing or too much, the procedures that are inflicted on the human body. If I went back into practice now, things like MRIs and CTs, you would have to be reoriented as to what is practical in this case or that. They have only come into use in the last ten years, and they are really a phenomenal contribution. The things you can do now! Things are at a point now that we would have never expected in 1940. The question still comes up about the need for all that expense.

I don't get to the hospital much anymore. I haven't gone to many medical meetings. Aside from my eye trouble, I have severe osteoarthritis of the spine, that has limited my involvement.

If I were in premed today and had my choice without worrying about money or anything, I would probably start on a program of scientific work of some kind. Research, I might have studied genetics. I don't know how successful I would be at it. But I don't think I would choose medicine.

Some of my most interesting cases involved the adrenal gland and thyroid disease. I remember a little girl who came into the clinic: she'd already been to a doctor in Minneapolis who hadn't been able to help her. We found out she had a pituitary gland tumor, and she went from a child with no energy to being a normal person. I can think of several cases like that. They're very satisfying when you think that some of them spent five or ten years before being diagnosed.

I made $12,000 my first year at the Duluth Clinic. I had worked for several years at a veterans hospital, and I was making $12,000 there too, but I got this chance to come to the Duluth Clinic, and I accepted right then. I knew several fellows who were working here, and it's been a very gratifying experience. Not everyone can say that, but most would want to say that.

≈

R Things are a lot different now than they were even twenty years ago. I advise you to take a real interest in your work, and you'll get a lot of satisfaction out of it. Work hard. You have so many possibilities. When you're young, if you want to be practical you have to go into something clinical. Look at the volume and demand.

68

VERNON A. HARRINGTON, M.D.
INTERNAL MEDICINE

I was born in Minneapolis and lived there through the tenth grade. Then we moved to Crosby where I graduated from high school. We lived on a farm, and prior to starting college, my father and I had a considerable disagreement. I wanted to be a lawyer, and he would have none of it, and so we compromised. I said I would take premed for a year and then reevaluate things. By the end of my first year, I had joined the naval reserve, so when I went on active duty, the officer said, "Premed, huh? Sign here."

My freshman year of medical school was an absolute nightmare. We carried a tremendous number of credits, I was in lab all day, and I didn't know if this was really for me. I was a very young kid, I was still only nineteen. My class was very young. I was out of medical school five years after I left high school. So at twenty two, I was a physician. That's pretty odd. We went to school year round. It wasn't much fun, we never did have a chance to take a summer vacation. But I found that when I started to get patient exposure, I just loved it. It made it a completely different experience for me. Of course I had no experience to call upon as a youngster as to what medicine was all about. I'd always been healthy and so had my family, but I was happy with my father's choice and the navy's.

Right after my internship at St. Mary's, I went into the service for a year. The day I left Great Lakes, the war started in Korea. I heard it on the radio as I drove out the gate. I went to Cleveland for two years for an internal medicine residency, and right after I started work at the Duluth Clinic, I went back in the service for a year and a half. I got out in 1954 and practiced until 1988.

There have been some huge advances. I think antibiotics would be the single most important thing. And more recently the fantastic technology with MRIs, CT scans, and heart-lung machines. I don't think I could have even envisioned anything like that when I was a fresh graduate. There's no doubt that they can significantly enhance life, but they can cause the loss of a lot of clinical skills that you had to have to practice in the old days—listening to chests, things like that. There are a lot of things that we did as a matter of conscience that really had a small return as far as clinical findings are concerned.

We will always remember our triumphs; we remember our failures too, but you don't want to talk about those. Sometimes they are pretty painful. I think every physician who practices has a disaster or two that he has to conclude were his fault. Fortunately, if you have a good relationship with people, they understand what you're feeling.

I remember a lady who came in with chest pain. She was on the table, and I was examining her. I started to examine the breast on the side she didn't have pain on, and she said, "No doctor, the pain is on the other side." Well, I found a cancer, and she had just had a mammogram six months earlier that was negative. Something like that makes you feel so good, to have been lucky enough to find it. Those are the things that give me more pleasure over the years than the esoteric things that occurred once in a blue moon.

If I could do it again, I'd love to. I'd love to come back and work here in Duluth. It's a marvelous field; every day is a complete new challenge. You never know, even from three in the afternoon, what that day is going to bring. It's an exciting field.

~

 R̥ *I think that, other than trying to keep up with things, which is tough, I am probably more abreast of what's going on in medicine now than when I was practicing because now I've got the time and I love it. And the most important thing in any field is to recognize one's limitations. I think young doctors often fear that if they suggest to a patient that they need some help, that patient will respect them less. And that's not true. The patients love it. They respect the person more for his willingness to say that he doesn't know everything, and they then have the opinion that they really have an honest person here. "If I need something more than what he can supply, he'll see that I get it." I'm sure that is the sequence that goes through people's minds.*

72

I was born in western Iowa in 1926. I grew up on a farm, the oldest of three children. I wanted to do something different; all I did was paint buildings or make hay and that was not what I wanted for the rest of my life.

My parents were influential, not as far as what I did, but in that they paid for college and medical school. As far as trying to get me to do this or that, absolutely not. In high school, I had an ingrown toenail, and I ended up with a leg that was infected with fifty-some boils. This was in the days before antibiotics. Our doctor was a relatively young man, and I got well. I think the care he gave me was what started my interest in medicine.

I had always wanted to go to Harvard, so at the end of my second year of medical school, I transferred back east where I graduated. I took all my internship and specialty training at Harvard before I came back to the Midwest. My wife and I were married after my first year of residency. We had no desire to stay in the East, so I joined a group of internists in Minneapolis. However they weren't looking for an associate; they were looking for a slave. Cy Brown asked me to come up and see the clinic. We did, we liked it, and I spent thirty-five happy years working there.

The most dramatic changes have occurred around cardiac surgery, due of course to better anesthesia and improved diagnostics. From an overall standpoint, with the introduction of antibiotics, you saw people you knew were going to die get well and go home. I don't think the technological advances are improving longevity. They may make it easier to make a diagnosis; we were making them too, but often working much harder at it. Personally, I think these tools are abused often. As new tools come out, doctors tend to forget that they can still take a history, do a physical exam, and get the same answer. They zero in on new things, sometimes to the exclusion of what they've learned in medical school. Maybe that seems like an old man preaching, but I think it's true. I think physicians should learn to be more selective about their use.

A lady came from the Upper Peninsula of Michigan who had significant emotional problems. We diagnosed hemochromatosis, an abnormal deposition of iron in a person's body, which usually leads to death. This woman had begun twenty-five years earlier to take some iron, and on the adage that if one was good, two were better, she finally got so that she was taking one to two hundred capsules a day. At that time the condition was rare because it was doubted that an increase of iron would cause problems, but nowadays we know very well that you can overwhelm the body with iron. And this was one of the first cases ever described.

We have three sons. We didn't urge them in any direction. They all felt that their father worked too hard, and they weren't going to make that mistake. They're all businessmen—working harder than I think I ever did.

Those early rounds? I'm a morning person, I grew up on a farm where we had to get up early. In training, we had to be on the floor and ready for rounds at seven o'clock. It was very rare that you went into a room and actually wakened a patient. They were invariably awake.

I'd do it again, sure. I don't think I'd become an internist again, I would go into genetics and genetic engineering. I think it's tremendously fascinating, and it may be the future as far as preventing cancer, birth defects, and other tragedies that occur early on.

In retirement, there is a sense of relief, at least for me. You miss the work, anyone who says they don't would be lying or kidding themselves. You miss the people, but not the long hours. Everyone said I would have an awful time adjusting. Not at all true. Within a week we went to Florida. I think it's much easier to pick up, quit, and leave.

R$_{\!x}$ *Be willing to work hard and expect long hours. Get involved in the politics of medicine in a positive manner. Save time for your family and for yourself. Be involved with your patients. The younger men seem to want to hold themselves more aloof from the patient than we did. That's a mistake. If you don't get to know your patient as a person, you've missed something out of your practice. Worrying about money can be an overriding concern, and then you've lost something out of life. For what it's worth, it's worth a lot.*

76

Roy R. Juntunen, M.D.
Family Medicine

Oh sure, I'm a native Minnesotan, born in Esko, December 1924, grew up and went to school there. I'm all Finnish; it was the Finnish Apostolic Lutheran Church that we belonged to, and it was very fundamental—no drinking, dancing, or movies. Card playing was not permitted, but we all played Rook because we didn't have to use regular cards. But the night my grandfather saw a cribbage board, he threw it in the stove because he felt it was gambling.

I decided I wanted to be a doctor in the service. I was in the army taking engineering, and my roommate said we could sign up for the medical aptitude test. I said, " I'm not interested." He said we'd get out of morning classes if we did it, and I became interested. Depending on grades, we were interviewed, and I was accepted. I went to premed at Vanderbilt University. Shortly after that they discontinued the engineering program, and all those guys ended up in the Battle of the Bulge.

I started medicine at the University of Pittsburgh, then transferred to Minnesota, and graduated in 1949. I came to St. Mary's for my internship in 1949–50. I practiced for a year and a half at Nashwauk, and then I went back in the army—the Korean War was on, and doctors were being drafted. I went back to Fort Sam Houston, and while there, I applied for transfer to the air force. I was married with two children at that time, and the first morning at Sam Houston they told us we were all going to Korea, which was understandable I suppose. After cajoling in headquarters, they allowed me to apply for transfer to the air force. I went to Kirkland Field in Albuquerque and was there until October 1953.

When I came out of the service I had no plans about where I was going. I talked to Dr. Carl Eklund, a classmate of mine, and he told me the West Duluth Clinic was looking for a doctor. So that's exactly how I got the job, and that's where I worked until retirement from 1953 to 1996.

I'm one of thirteen kids. My mother was very encouraging, she was always the more academic of the two. But my dad wasn't too keen. When I came home and told him, "It looks like I'm going into medicine," he said, "Well, I probably wouldn't if I were you, but I'll help you all I can." And he did indeed. When you're one of thirteen, it's a sacrifice for them to help.

It's hard to pick out one specific case. When you look back on your past there tends to be just a blur. The first year in practice, I delivered triplets, three boys. It was quite a circus because I had heard fetal heart tones and was expecting twins. In those days, we didn't do X rays or anything, women just went into labor and then you found out what happened. I had to go after the second twin. I was feeling all kinds of legs and arms and I am wondering why am I having so much trouble getting my bearings here? I got to two feet, and I delivered the child, and then I thought now we'll get the placenta and out came a third one.

The imaging that came along, MRIs and CAT scans, the lab work and tests, those are the big advances. Making a diagnosis was so haphazard prior to that. I used to scrub in a lot with A. O. Swenson, and I can remember that many times you'd go in on a so-called acute abdomen when you didn't know the diagnosis. You found the diagnosis when you opened up. Now, of course, they have a much better idea.

Go through medicine again? I don't know. I think if you're going to go into it, you should be real dedicated. And I will say that I felt pretty secure with myself, I worked within myself, you know. I originally went into it on account of this devious route. The funny thing is in my high school annual where they predict what you're going to do, they predicted that I'd be a doctor. I couldn't imagine that. I said, how wrong can they be?

I thought the generation ahead of us practiced during the best years, the ones that graduated in the twenties. There was no paperwork to speak of; they were respected in their communities; and they weren't taxed very heavily. It was a freer life, no rules and regulations. But medicine was tougher too, they all worked hard and never took any time off. It was hand-to-hand combat.

≈

 ℞ *No matter who you are, you're going to hit times when symptoms are so confused that you don't really know where to go. You may be apprehensive, but as you get into it, you'll enjoy it more.*

80

PHILIP L'ABBE, M.D.
ANESTHESIOLOGY

I am the oldest of three, born in Prince Albert, Ontario, Canada, which is now Thunder Bay. I went to high school there, then to the University of Toronto, and graduated from medical school in 1955. I interned in Bridgeport, Connecticut, went back to Canada and into a general practice for two years in North Bay, Ontario, which I really didn't want to do. But I was married and had children and was kind of forced into it. And then after two years we left, and I went to the University of Minnesota. I did my residency in anesthesiology, and we didn't quite make it back to Canada; we ended up in Duluth.

When we left Canada, we had taken out permanent visas. We first came down on a student visa, and you couldn't work, so we weren't sure what we were going to do. In 1970, Dr. Latterell was here, and I came up and talked to him. I didn't really want to go back to Canada. So we stayed; we were here twenty-nine years, from 1960 to 1989. There were three of us; Dr. Boecker came a few months before I did, and we were three until 1974. It was a long time, a lot of call. Of course, when someone was gone, we were on call every other night.

Retirement is great. We've had a place in Florida since 1980, a little condo down there. We had a target date of 1990, said that would be my finishing date. But actually I quit a year earlier.

There probably wasn't as much surgery in those days as there is now.

But we were on call a lot more often. If you were up all night, you still had to work the next day, so we always tried to get the man on call out of there by one o'clock in the afternoon. Most surgeons in the sixties and the early seventies went to their offices every day. So they all wanted to get their surgery done in the early afternoon. Early on, if we worked until two or two-thirty, it was a late day. In the last fifteen years, it hasn't been like that at all. It just goes on and on and on.

Really, advances don't suddenly appear. Any changes you see are very gradual. There is no sudden demarcation, where all of a sudden things are better. As far as the practice of anesthesiology is concerned, new drugs came along: newer inhalation agents, IV agents, and muscle relaxants, but medicine really doesn't change that dramatically, it evolves gradually. Things that are tried and found to be worthwhile are kept, and things that aren't are not used any more.

I remember the teenager who shot herself in the confessional up at Marshall School. She shot herself through the chest and was taken to the emergency room. They put in a central line and took her right up to the operating room because she was bleeding quite profusely. I pumped blood into her, but it didn't seem to be doing any good. We got the chest open, and the central line was in the chest cavity, so all the blood I was pumping into her was running into her chest. We put in a second line; I didn't think she was going to make it, but she did.

We used ether in the beginning, then Halthane came out and replaced ether. Ether was an explosive anesthetic, and of course, if you're using an explosive, you can't use electrocautery.

Oh yes, I'd become a doctor again. My wife and I have seven children, but none of them are doctors. They thought I was gone a lot when they were younger. When they were growing up, a lot of times I didn't see them in the morning before they went to school, and by the time I got home, they were in bed. I'm afraid a lot of the child rearing was left to my wife.

The paperwork had already started by the time I left. It was just unbelievable the way it increased. And the government rules and regulations and so forth—I don't miss any of that. I still get the ASA newsletter—all the dealings with government and so forth—it's very discouraging. I'm glad I'm not there. I think we practiced during an era that has passed. After 1980, you gradually started seeing the decline.

∾

 R_X *Pick the part of the country you want to live in. Most anesthesiologists in this country are in groups. I think it's nice to have a group, but you have to be compatible because you are a fairly close-knit organization. It's important that you're going to be able to get along with your associates and the type of anesthesia that they're practicing.*

84

JOSEPH H. LEEK, M.D.
OTOLARYNGOLOGY

I was born in 1923 in Denver, Colorado, and had no real home. I was in a family where my father, because of the depression, moved from city to city. I went to fourteen schools before I got to college. I had no home really until I came to Duluth. From the age of ten, I decided I wanted to be a surgeon; health, science, illness, and surgery all came together for me early.

I graduated from school in Benton Harbor, Michigan, went to the University of Michigan, and got my M.D. there in 1948. My internship and residency were both at the University of Chicago. I finished in 1952. Dr. O'Neill from the Duluth Clinic came down. I listened to his story and liked him as a person, so I said I would come up. It was winter; there was snow on the ground and I thought, my God, what am I doing in this part of the world? But I met the clinic doctors, and I visited the building and St. Mary's. I had already decided I wanted to be in a collegial partnership of all specialties, and so that's why I came here. I served in the military during World War II and again during the Korean War and came back in 1955.

Between my junior and senior year, I worked as an extern in a hospital in Chicago. I was going past the operating room when I heard this male voice singing. I looked through the window, and I could see the doctor, the nurse, and the patient. It was obvious the surgeon was doing the singing. I went to the head nurse and said, "That surgeon's singing," and she said, "He's very happy, and he likes to sing to his patients because they're under general anesthesia."

85

And I thought, isn't it wonderful to enjoy your work so much and have so much fun at it? I asked to meet him. He told me about ENT and arranged for me to get into the University of Chicago. I was just lucky, all because of that very unusual story. And I've never regretted it, honestly.

The most patients I ever saw in a single day was eighty-two. In the mornings I'd do surgery and then see patients in the afternoon. My first year I made $8,000. From 1958–63 I was the only ENT doctor in Duluth, on call every day, all the traumas and foreign bodies, that was my work. During this time, my poor wife took care of seven kids. She understood that I was married to a profession as well as to her. Things are different today, but in the old days that's the way it was. All of us old-timers were built to do that kind of work. And the spouses, hard as it was (and today it would be unacceptable), they took it. We have seven children, a couple of doctorates but no M.D.s.

The greatest advance for my patients was the operating microscope. I was the first doctor in Minnesota to do a stapedectomy, and it's because of the operating microscope that surgery can be done. The second most important was the latex surgical glove. It was the disposable, thin, skintight glove that helped enormously our dexterity to work in the ear.

I remember one case I published where the facial nerve, which is always in the area when I do a stapedectomy, was in my way during the operation. I was trying to get it away from my field and was about to cut it when I realized it was an anomaly and fortunately, didn't cut. I went out to tell her husband and he said, "I'll see you in court, Doctor." I wrote that up, saying, "Be alert, it can be in the wrong pew, don't cut it."

I'm still employed; I still see patients, and I have my administrative job. I do exactly what I want to do all the time, for the most part I always have.

Would I again? Absolutely, in a minute. I would never think about any field but surgery. And if I were lucky, I'd go back into ENT, absolutely. We have a longer life; we don't burn out; our field is gentler, I guess.

Physicians contributed to the current problems in medical care certainly, but not alone. Patients did. Biotechnology did. Hospitals did. Lawyers did. Insurance did. And government and big business and unions did. All of us in one way or another have contributed to what is wrong today.

Scarce resources will decide our futures, the law of supply and demand. The younger members of my profession have more ways to sustain life and are reimbursed by the system to use them without regard for the bill. And if they don't use them and something adverse occurs, they will be sued. That's different from the way we lived. The younger doctor has a whole different stage to play on, so you have to be very sympathetic.

≈

 ℞ *It's a wonderful profession, you will be utterly fulfilled with the pleasure of serving; just find the right specialty that you can work in.*

88

HAROLD B. LEPPINK, M.D.
FAMILY MEDICINE, PUBLIC HEALTH

I decided to become a physician in about thirty minutes in my life. A recruiting officer asked me what program I wanted to be in. He listed thirteen, and when I said I didn't know, he said, "Go sit in the hall and think about it." So I did. My neighbor was a dentist, a funny old fellow, so I came back in and said dentistry. He said, "The navy premed and predental contracts are identical, but if you choose medicine, we'll have you in school in three weeks." I said, "Sign me up for medicine." There it was. It took about thirty minutes to make the decision, and I have never regretted it for a minute. I have had an absolutely wonderful career, never a moment of regret. I finished my internship in Detroit just as the Korean War was starting, and I didn't want to be any part of it, so I put in as a conscientious objector. I offered to go to Korea as a public health physician. Someone in the State Department who was a member of the Church of the Brethren heard about that and wrote me. The Brethren were looking for someone to run their clinics in Puerto Rico, and after an interview, they offered my wife and me both a job. That was probably the most significant thing I've done in my life. It molded me, defined my social philosophy.

When we came home, I thought I wanted to be a surgeon and went to Milwaukee County Hospital for a residency. I didn't like it, but I took the first year. For the second year, the chief of surgery suggested I try pathology, anesthesia, and some of the specialty surgeries. I did and it was great, a very good year. Then I researched places where I could practice prepaid medicine and started visiting them. We came to Two Harbors in 1956, liked the people and the doctors, and they practiced prepaid medicine side by side with fee-for-service medicine. That worked out well; I was there for thirteen years, and then got tired of practicing.

I had always had this idea of being involved in administration and public health. So I quit practice in 1970 and went to the university to get my master's degree in public health, the same year my oldest daughter entered Hamline. When I came back to Duluth, I didn't have a job; my predecessor asked me to take a contract with St. Louis County to close down Nopeming Sanitorium and put TB in the mainstream of medical care. That project was very successful. And then, in my second career move in twenty years, I was made health officer for St. Louis County. My interest was noncommunicable disease. I realized that one reason we did so little was that people didn't know what to do, and we didn't have any tools to do it with. I told the board that's what I wanted to work on and they were very supportive.

The multiple risk factor concept has changed everything—people's attitudes toward exercise, nutrition, smoking cessation, seat belt use: the whole concept was born at this time. Now we didn't have to accept disease as the inevitable consequence of aging, there wasn't any reason why people couldn't live longer and better. We could combine nutrition and medication and exercise and a number of factors and parlay that into increased longevity.

R_X *I was in the profession for almost forty-five years, and it has provided a tremendous amount of satisfaction. Doctors aren't perfect, they aren't gods. When it comes to sickness and disease and death, people want someone there in charge of the situation. We elevate people and place a mantle on them to make decisions relative to life and death. This is the obligation society puts on you and therefore calls you by the title "doctor." And it expects something in return.*

92

NIILO E. LEPPO, M.D.
PEDIATRICS

In high school, I was interested in three things—architecture, medicine, and the navy. My sister was going with a handsome naval officer. I liked him, but I chose medicine.

I went to the University of Helsinki and studied for seven years, interning in communicable diseases. I graduated in 1936 and then was invited by the Rockefeller Foundation to study in America, maternal-child health. I couldn't resist, and I also got a degree in public health.

When the war came, I was finishing my studies. I was married now to a young lady from Finland, and we went back there. I was sent that first winter to the border areas—it was so cold. When the Finns made a treaty with the Russians, I went back to my health department. The last year of the war, I spent in Petrozavodsk, which is much discussed here as our sister city.

After the war I was the community health officer for Helsinki. We organized a program for public health nurses and midwives and built five hundred health centers. I started well-baby clinics and maternity clinics and our infant mortality rate dropped to the lowest in the world. And our public education is tremendous—there are no illiterate people in Finland.

Soon the state health department called me into their service. Medical directors worldwide came to see our program because we had one of the best public health departments in Europe. I was asked by the World

Health Organization to work with them. I worked there eighteen months and got their program going strong. Then the people of South Korea asked would anyone volunteer to help us? I said, "I am getting tired of this paperwork and no fun time with my babies. I'll go." Nobody knew anything about Korea. We landed in a snowbank. I worked there six months with seed money from the UN, but I didn't get anything going before North Korea attacked.

I came to Minnesota to train at the Mayo Clinic. There were two Duluth boys among the students, and they said, "You would love it in Duluth, excellent hunting and fishing." So I said, "Let's go!"

I came to Duluth in July 1953. I was forty-four years old, too old for some. I had a very interesting and illustrious career, but I was eager to get back to my babies. I talked with Dr. Buckley, and he said, "Why don't you come with us? We'd like a third fellow." So I did. There are wonderful doctors in Duluth. The retired doctors still get together and talk about the good olden times, but we're happy we don't have to practice anymore.

Many, many remarkable stories. They called me to come and see a child with a fever. At that time we still made house calls. I would always look at their throat and in their ears and listen to their lungs. And I always felt their tummies in case I would occasionally find something of interest. There was lots of resistance in the lower abdomen. I thought it was the child's bladder so we had her go potty. That looked normal, and the mass hadn't gotten any smaller. We took the child to the hospital, and on the X ray you could see little bones and teeth. We opened her up, and there was a lemon-sized tumor coming out of one of her ovaries—a teratoma, the parts of another baby inside of her. Very rare, I have seen only one other case.

I have been very lucky, very happy in my practice. I have traveled around the world, but I was very happy in Duluth. The young mothers and dear babies—it keeps an old grandpa young.

R̶x̶ *Medicine is a fine, fine profession. It depends a little on which field you go into. Americans, especially, tend toward subspecialties. Advanced technologies are good to have in problem cases, but in pediatrics those are a very small minority. In most cases, I prefer the simple tests, and I practiced for thirty-two years.*

96

HORST G. MAY, M.D.
ANESTHESIOLOGIST

I was born in Germany and went to school there. During World War II, I was in the German army in Russia. Six months after the end of the war, medical school opened, and my grandmother said, "Why don't you become a doctor? You've been lying around here long enough." I said "Yes, why not?" If she had said "Why don't you study to be a minister?" I would have done it. I think I could have enjoyed anything once I made up my mind. As a veteran, I didn't have to pay for medical school, and when I finished my grandmother said, "Why don't you go to America?" and again I said, "Why not?" I even brought my own Volkswagen. In 1955, I went to Madison, and during my third year there I got married and decided to stay.

When I decided to go into anesthesia, I took two years training in Minneapolis, but I couldn't get a license in Minnesota because foreign medical schools were not approved at that time. I could get a license for Illinois though, so I went there and stayed for nine years. I always wanted to come back to Minnesota; I liked the lakes—the big lake—and the remoteness of Minnesota. I had a friend who finished anesthesia one year ahead of me, Bernie Boecker, and I stayed in touch with him. In 1969, St. Luke's needed another anesthesiologist and by that time, I could finally get a license for Minnesota. I met with the board of medical examiners, and they asked me why I'd like to go to Minnesota. I looked at their name tags, names like Rasmussen, Gustafson, Gunderson, Peterson. And I said "I'd like my children to grow up in a Nordic environment." That was it. Approved! And so I came here. And when I turned sixty-five in 1989, I thought well, that's it. Now I quit. I was in good shape, in good health. And I haven't regretted it since.

Medicine wasn't the great love of my life. That would have been being a forest ranger or an airline pilot. But there were no airplanes flying for a long time after the war. So I thought, whatever I do, I'll do it right. And I liked it as I went on, and I thought I did a good job.

The advent of narcotics, the idea that you could give a narcotic that was cardiovascularly friendly was a tremendous achievement from the standpoint of safety. We used ether, which was explosive, and flourothane, which affected the liver, and pentothal, which sometimes depressed the circulation, and nitrous oxide that wasn't potent enough. There had to be something else. Doctors started experimenting with high doses of narcotics, doing a whole operation with morphine and nitrous oxide. Like the name says, it will induce sleep, because Morpheus is the Greek god of sleep. A Swiss pharmacist named the drug. In those days, doctors had an education before they went into medicine. Today they don't have an education; they go to medical school and get trained. Knowing the Greek gods is one difference between education and training. An education involves the whole person and training, just a limited sector of a person's capacity.

I knew all the giants who were setting the direction of medicine in Duluth and Superior when I came here. Now they're retired, and some are gone. I see the ones who are in the prime of their lives now, and I know that they'll be old someday. I'm still around and I see all that, how it happens.

In 1969, my first night on call, I had a tracheal-esophageal fistula in a newborn. They are tricky because you have to share—you have your ET tube there, and the surgeon has to work around it. But it went well. That child came back for a tonsillectomy, and I thought, look at that—I still remember that night. At seventeen, she came back for an appendectomy, and again I remembered her. She came in for a C-section, and that I remember. Five years ago, I got a call from a young girl asking if I would like to buy an Advent wreath. I said, "How do you know who I am?" and she said, "You were there when I was born." I realized she was the child who had been the C-section nine years before.

~

℞ *Be compassionate. Everything else you can learn. Imagine yourself being on the other side, realize what it feels like to be a patient. Remember, someday you will be on the receiving end. Someday, as sure as the Mississippi flows from north to south, you will have to take some of your own medicine. Remember, too, that it is a gift from the Chief of Staff up there that you can practice medicine. And be a good listener. Try to create the impression that you're not in a hurry—even if you are.*

One time as a child I was very sick. Doc George came out and said, "Well, this boy is going to die if I don't operate on him tonight." I always remember that vividly because for some reason I didn't want a scar, so when I was being put to sleep, I told them I didn't want a scar and he said, "There'll be no scar at all." Well, I had the worst scar I've ever seen in my whole life. They used ether to put you to sleep in those days, and you had nightmares. To this day, I can remember the nightmares, falling and empty space forever. But I survived. And I decided at that age to be a doctor.

My parents were encouraging, but I had a sister, and they were of the opinion that their daughter had to be educated too. I spent my service time in Germany, and when I came out I used the GI bill to attend the University of Rochester, then medical school, then my residency at the University of North Carolina, Chapel Hill. Then back to Rochester for two years, then New York State-Syracuse for two years, so I had six years of training. When I looked here in Duluth, everyone felt that this was a depressed area but that the taconite amendment would pass and things would improve. I was married and had two children when I moved here in 1960. I liked the fact that there was a clinic group and a nonclinic group, and yet they were working together. You could be a member of all the hospitals in town and have the opportunity to know everybody. That was one thing that sold me on this place. Plus it was near the outdoors.

I started at the West Duluth Clinic and practiced there for thirty years.

I became chief surgeon of the DM&IR railroad in 1962, and I did that in addition to my general surgery.

I think you realize later in practice how long it takes to become really mature. I remember doctors that were older than I that would see a dying patient and if they were sleeping, would go right on and never wake them up. After I matured, I was always careful if a patient of mine was dying to stop and wake them up to talk to them. Because when you're immature you want to slough those. You have nothing—what can you tell this man who's dying? But he needs your support more than anyone else, more than all your patients. And so I always made an effort to relate to my patients and tried to anticipate their needs. That was one thing I felt as a surgeon most surgeons fail to do. It was a hard part of surgery, to see someone who was going to die and there was nothing you could do for them. I always remember the many people I did that with, how much it improved their outlook in the last few weeks of life.

You have many cases, and the ones I remember are those where I felt I matured more, not just because I was such a fantastic surgeon (although I think I was!). A man who was an alcoholic came in with G.I. bleeding. After two or three episodes, I went in and did a shunt, and he was real sick. He had been divorced and had two girls, and he didn't know where they were. Afterwards, I got a call that his former wife and his daughters were there and would like to talk to me. And there they were, lovely people and really concerned about what was happening to him. And you realize that you've got to be careful when you peg someone as to who they are. My opinion, and everyone else's, was that no one gave a damn what was going to happen to him. You realize that a lot of time people have failed in the way they deal with life, but there are still people out there that love them and want them to live.

I thought at first I might miss the companionship of other doctors, but I find that I enjoy being able to have the hours to do what I want to do. I don't think life is full of enjoyment every second. I don't think we can have life that way. And so you do the things that you never had the time to do.

When I first came here I was on call every night and every weekend. I had six children, but they just said there was no way they wanted that life.

~

℞ *You should go where you will enjoy working and be the type of person that enjoys people and wants to go where people are in need. Make up your mind what you want out of your own life; if your expectations aren't too high, you're going to have a wonderful life. If you do have high expectations, you will never be happy because you never will have enough. I think we lose sight of the fact that in America we have a good life. For tomorrow, a family practitioner is ideal, they are going to be held in high esteem.*

104

I was born in Alabama in 1926. My parents were Danish and went back to Denmark twice during the Depression. We moved back for good when I was five years old. I stayed there until the spring of 1940, after the German occupation. I went through the seventh grade. My father was a civil engineer working in Venezuela, and my mother was visiting him when Denmark was occupied. So my sister and I joined them in this tiny village on the coast, and my mother taught us. After a year, they decided to send me to the States to school. They had friends in Montgomery, and I stayed with them for a year and then went to boarding school. My sister stayed in Venezuela with my parents, and my mother kept teaching her. After high school, I went back because I hadn't seen them for three years. I joined them in Caracas, and I taught my sister for a year. Then I came back to college at the University of Richmond in Virginia, and I graduated from there in 1949.

The year I was back in Venezuela my mother had asked me what I'd like to be, and I said I'd like to be a nurse. She said, "How about a doctor," and I thought that would be wonderful, so that was settled there and then. I had always been interested in everything in that direction, enjoyed biology and things like that.

After I graduated from the university, I took a general internal medicine internship in Chicago, and that's where I met my husband. I went back to Richmond for a medical residency, and he came up and proposed. The following year I was back in Chicago, and we were married in 1955.

We had four children in less than four years. I took some years off and stayed home with the children. I don't think that it was ideal; you get out of touch with a lot of it, and things progress even though you keep reading. It's not the same as being right in the middle of it, but it worked out. I worked at the free clinic at Miller Dwan; I took care of the internal medicine section once a week. And I worked for Dr. Harrington; he went to Florida twice a year and I'd take care of his patients, which was good experience. After that I worked part-time at the clinic, and I continued to work there more and more. As far as practicing was concerned, I didn't think being a woman was a problem, but I didn't take call because I figured I couldn't handle both the family and patients.

I've had lots of interesting cases. I remember a man who had tertiary syphilis with a huge aortic aneurysm; it had eroded through his ribs, and we got to see it up close. He was a nice old gentleman; he worried about what a mess it was going to be if it went suddenly. It ruptured into his bronchi rather than to the outside, but the effect was the same. I suppose that at that stage we couldn't have operated on it even nowadays. Nowadays we don't see much in the way of syphilis, but at that time, in the South, there was plenty of it. Penicillin was still in its youth.

There have been so many advancements. I think the eradication of smallpox and the finding of the polio vaccine were two wonderful events. I remember the polio epidemic, it was terrible. The advances in cardiac

106

surgery. The advances in various diagnostic treatments. There's so much, medicine evolves constantly. So many wonderful drugs, antibiotics, the medications we have for hypertension. Transplantation surgery and vascular surgery, there is so much.

I would do it again, yes, definitely. I've enjoyed it. We have two children who are physicians, but we tried not to push them into medicine. Some of the most unhappy people I've seen were students whose parents or whose father was a physician and who were expected to become physicians. So we tried to sit on our hands. And I think they are both happy about their decision.

I retired in 1991. It's strange, actually. I missed my work very much; it took me about a year to adjust. It was like going through a mourning. And I didn't expect that. I have to stay busy and enjoy life. I think it was the right time to do it, but it was tough to say good-bye to it.

R︎x *Enjoy it. Keep learning. It was a wonderful field to work in, always something new and different. Each person has to solve their own problems, I don't think we can give a lot of advice.*

108

I remember my scoutmaster, Dr. Miller, who was a professor of anatomy. He'd show me around the anatomy building after school, and that got my curiosity up. My father had a degree in engineering and was on the faculty of the University of Minnesota. His friend, a professor of biochemistry, said, "The thing for you to do is to go into biochemistry, get your Ph.D., and then get your M.D." So I majored in chemistry at the University of Minnesota which was fine, but it included needing to do physics. When I got to electricity, I could not figure out what they were talking about, so I switched out of chemistry and continued on with premed. I was accepted into medical school at the University of Minnesota and finished in 1943.

It was wartime, and I became a lieutenant in the medical corps. In 1944, I was in England in a special unit trained for gas casualties. The military felt gas would be used after the invasion of the Rhine, and we didn't have a plan for dealing with it. I learned about compounds used in gas warfare, including things like nitrogen mustard. I didn't see any reason to know this except they said it was important, and so I learned about it.

When I came back, I took an internal medicine residency in Detroit at Wayne County Hospital where I had interned. There was a hematologist there that I became assigned to, and I also had a mentor in hematopathology. I became a hematology fellow, doing projects involving a new, unused drug called nitrogen mustard. Of the patients at this hospital, there were about four thousand chronically ill and indigent, a lot of people I could work with. Many of them had cancers of various kinds and leukemias. Researching with nitrogen mustard, we could figure out advisable doses, see what it did to tumor and bone marrow, and determine how much they could stand.

In my fourth year, I was chief medical resident and was thinking of staying in Detroit, but I thought about my lakes and streams and trees in Minnesota. I knew of the Duluth Clinic, they were well-known from Dr. Tuohy and his influence. It was a superior grade of medicine here, so we decided on Duluth. I was one of twenty-five physicians when I joined the clinic, the sixth internist. And I practiced from 1950 to 1982.

I think of a Cloquet family who had twin daughters, four years old. One of them became leukemic, the other one seemed all right. In those days, working with the drugs we had, the leukemic child got better but didn't get well because we didn't know how to get them well. Talking with Dr. Aufderheide, we thought about a program just coming into the publications from a physician who was doing bone marrow transplants. We didn't really know how to do this; I had read only one article about it. We arranged to give her radiation and a large dose of bone marrow extracted from her sister. Dr. Aufderheide was looking over my shoulder, and Dr. McNutt's radiology machine was shining on this child who was lying on the floor getting a big dose. By tracking a variant cell type, we were able to determine that the bone marrow did grow in the child, but then the leukemia overtook it anyway. We didn't win that one, but it was the first bone marrow transplant done here.

The hematologic and oncology patterns of my life turned out to be big-growing, big-changing things. I guess I was the only one in town active in hematology because nobody else seemed to be doing it. The field of oncology started to grow, and in the sixties, working with drugs for various cancers, we began to do a little better. Many survived that wouldn't have in earlier days. When I retired, I left behind six brave young oncologists. Sure, I'd do it again. Medicine is a great field of interesting things to do.

For a while, retirement is a problem. There is some emptiness because you miss the familiar pattern. Neither my wife or I knew how to golf when I retired. We still don't, but we keep trying.

℞ *Work hard. Try to take care of people. Do the things that they need, not what the insurance companies or bureaucrats think you should do. And don't worry about economics. If you do a good job, you'll be alright. I go back to that internal medicine training in the county hospital as an example. There was nobody telling us we couldn't work on all those patients with investigational drugs. We didn't have to have our forms signed. We just said, "Okay, here's a chance to get better, and we're going to do the best we can." They said, "Okay!" and on you go.*

JAMES E. MUNGER, M.D.
FAMILY MEDICINE

Our family moved to Delaware when I was very young. My grandfather was a doctor in South St. Paul; I was born in Minneapolis, but I never knew him. I guess he was an influence though because as far back as I can remember, I wanted to be a physician.

My parents encouraged us in our education, but not in one area or another. I went to Auburn College, then Ohio State University. I got married during my junior year in medical school, and spent two years in the navy in Norfolk. Out of the navy and before I had made any decisions about where to go, we got a call to come to Duluth to the American Steel and Wire Works, which was the steel plant. While I was in medical school, I had worked at one of the big companies in Columbus in the emergency room at night. The doctor who had been in charge of that recommended me to United States Steel and from there I came up to be the first full-time doctor at the steel plant.

That was in 1957, and I stayed until 1963. At one time there were 3,000 employees at the steel plant. Occupational medicine and the plant physician were becoming more important, more critical, so that while I was there I was overseeing the care of injuries and becoming very safety conscious. We did have a few severe accidents, but very few. The safety record was excellent. I was there full-time, on call twenty-four hours a day, seven days a week. We had two hospital beds in the dispensary and twenty-four hour R.N. coverage with Isabelle Malkovich and Mary Schubitz. The injuries that went to the hospital were bad ones, otherwise they stayed.

I got disillusioned with corporate medicine when you couldn't just do your job. That's when I went into private practice. I went into practice in Kenwood by myself. In those days, if you didn't join a group there wasn't anywhere to go, so I stayed solo for several years and shared call. That was hard; if you were alone, you might only get half a day without call. I got into the health service at UMD, a part-time position, but gradually the number of hours I spent there increased, and then I was appointed full-time until retirement.

I don't know if you'd say times have changed, I guess one grows with the times. My main interest was family practice, so I did a little bit of everything. The intensive care units would be one element of improvement and antibiotics, that's obvious. And rehabilitation—even realizing that rehabilitation was possible. One of the big changes over the years was that the solo practitioner became nonexistent. And the increased paperwork, the government regulation. When we started practice, all the hospitals had review committees, and we worked at maintaining and improving the quality of care. It was ingrained in us that if we were going to be physicians, if we were going to be involved in the profession, we had to make it the best we knew how. Probably beats the paperwork. I've heard more and more doctors say that medicine is no longer fun. I'm sure you've heard that before.

My wife and I had three children, but none of them became involved in medicine.

One of the satisfactions of general medicine was contact with the family. I had a patient who was one hundred years old and in the hospital only very briefly when he died. The same day he died, I delivered a newborn. It was that sort of continuity that was very satisfying. You'd have to change gears from geriatrics to obstetrics; it kept things interesting and kept you on your toes.

In the early years, the physicians had a more relaxed relationship with each other. Residents in the last few years gave me the impression that they were driven to go as fast as they could; they didn't seem to have time to sit down and talk to their patients. It is more a business than it used to be.

My practice was during the days when it was about the best, when some of the best things were happening. Your doctor was an advisor, a lot of things.

~

R̲x̲ *There aren't many new things under the sun when you think about it. Be interested in enough things going on around you so that you're active in things other than medicine. Because when you retire, if you haven't got something else that interests you, you just go off to Arizona and play golf. I personally can't imagine anybody who just does nothing but play golf. I used to say to people in the steel plant that you've got to retire TO something, don't retire FROM something.*

116

George F. Nisius, M.D.
Obstetrics, Gynecology

I was born in Clinton, Ohio, in 1915. And I had medicine in mind from the very beginning. My parents more or less let us do whatever we wanted. I did a surgery residency in Chicago, and a fellow in the department mentioned Duluth. I got an interview, liked the place, and decided to come up. We got here on New Year's Eve in 1951, and I was supposed to start work the following day. We didn't have any furniture; we didn't know anybody in town. We had an opportunity to locate in Cleveland or Chicago, but we liked the people, and we liked the doctors at the clinic, they were so efficient and well-trained. There were twenty-three there when I started, so I was the twenty-fourth. I had never been in a small town until Duluth, never seen snow like this before. They used to kid me because I had knobby snow tires. I had gotten my Sears and Roebuck chains out at the same time I moved to Duluth.

I was a little older than most doctors. I came here after a year of internship, five years of residency, one year of general practice, and four years in the air force. So I wasn't too young then.

I went to high school in Cleveland, college in Brey, Ohio, and medical school at Loyola University in Chicago. After I graduated in 1941, I started as a surgical resident, but was then called to active duty in the air force and served four years as a flight surgeon. When I came back I still had six months before I was board eligible, so I went into general practice for a year.

When I came up here, they were a little surprised that I was interested in a small town. But I practiced for thirty years here. The people are so pleasant, the climate is good, and it's so clean.

There have been one or two fundamental changes that occurred one at a time, just brought in gradually. You can visualize the infant and scan to determine pelvic capacity, so now you're not running into that many problems with childbirth. One of the detrimental things was we talked so much about the advances that every mother thinks she should have a perfectly normal, healthy baby. But there are hereditary factors and other things to be considered. We just cannot guarantee it. If they don't get it, you wind up in court. I think that's one of the biggest changes in obstetrics, so many people are refusing to do it.

Of course, for an obstetrician, just a baby being born is amazing!

There is one unusual case I recall, and there is no explanation for it. I operated on a young woman who had cancer of the ovary, to tell what her prognosis would be. The surgery was to take out both ovaries and the uterus and to clean out the pelvis. When I operated, I found she had metastatic disease all over her abdomen. I thought she'd live two months, three at the most. She lived fifteen years. That's what we used to call host resistance.

For the first eight years I was here, there were only two of us. Took call every other night, six o'clock at night until six o'clock in the morning and every other weekend, Friday night to Monday morning. You didn't come home, you just stayed in the hospital. Obstetrics was rather difficult in those days. After all those years of call, I got tired of it. So retirement wasn't so hard. I've enjoyed my retirement.

I'd become a doctor again. I think we gave good care; I'm sure we did. They don't give as much personalized care now as we did then. Younger people are not used to the personalized care that the older generation was used to—docs who would hold your hand and talk to you. I think the objection most people have is that my doctor doesn't talk to me. Personalization has been taken out, and the overall practice of medicine has suffered.

Sometimes the doctors are at fault—I'm not excusing the doctors. Some are too brusque and don't explain well. They see their associates use the same format. They're not trying to get away from their patients; it's just that they haven't been trained to do that kind of thing. And they can't see the usefulness of it. A good general practitioner will end up practicing psychiatry, too.

≈

R̟ *Go with a group. I enjoyed private practice except for all the bookkeeping, medical records, too much business. It was very, very convenient to have all the specialties covered in the same building.*

120

ALBERT L. NISSWANDT, M.D.
NEUROSURGERY, EMERGENCY MEDICINE

I was the fifth child of seven, born in St. Paul in 1925. I was raised on Payne Avenue, and anybody that grew up on the East Side thought the whole world was Swedish and Lutheran. They were so shocked when they wandered eight blocks away and found that there were other people in the world.

My mother and father each had a very limited education; my father went to the third grade in Sweden and then stayed home to work, and my mother the same. I never finished high school; I worked for awhile and then joined the United States Marine Corps. And due to my great intellectual ability I was put in the infantry. I was involved in the landings on a few Pacific islands and was wounded on Saipan in 1944.

Not being a high school graduate, I didn't go far in the service. When I got out, I decided that one must have a slip of paper to show people in life or your chances are limited, so I started college at the University of Minnesota. I had no interest in medicine; a friend talked me into going into premed. Unfortunately he didn't get into med school and I did, but he didn't hold it against me. I interned at Cook County in Chicago, during which I got married. I was in family practice for a year in St. Paul and then started a neurosurgical residency at the Mayo Clinic.

After that, we traveled to California, and I practiced for a year. But Minnesota seemed more suited to my style of existence; I liked the water and the lake. So we moved back to Duluth and have been here ever since.

Dr. Pollard was practicing alone at that time, and I joined him; later we were joined by Dr. Bullock. I'm not sure what we called ourselves; there were no public relations men in those days. We were on call literally thirteen out of fourteen days, year after year with no rest, up every night. Back then there were no neurologists in town; we did all the neurology, all the neurosurgery, but it's okay when you're young and love your work.

The trio dissolved in 1967, and Dr. Bullock and I joined the Duluth Clinic where I practiced until 1975. Then I started practice in the emergency room at St. Mary's Hospital. All of my transitions have been difficult; I don't think I've felt completely qualified for any job I've had in life, but I felt very productive in the emergency room—I had a marvelous experience.

One case that always comes to mind was the four-year-old who fell off the fence. I happened to be outside the elevator when a stretcher was wheeled into pediatrics, and there was a four year old from Hibbing with fixed, dilated pupils, arched back, ready to breathe his last. We rushed the child into surgery without undressing him, and Dr. L'Abbe put an endotracheal tube in without anesthetic since the child was in a deep coma. We took a chance, shaved the right side of the head, and turned the bone flap within eight minutes. We found a huge epidural blood clot, which we removed and closed it up. The child recovered and left the hospital in one week, perfectly normal. It was a miracle. Nowadays that child would not live because we would have to go to X ray or MRI or CAT scans and we could not rush into surgery on limited knowledge. By the time the tests were done, the child would have irreversible brain damage. They are great advances, but not as a fishing expedition.

Most of the time, when you wake up at three in the morning, you've just had a dream that you're in surgery and you can't stop the bleeding and everything is going wrong, but occasionally you're in surgery at three, and it's miraculous.

I've been very happy with medicine. Three of my seven children went into medicine, all in primary care. They saw me running day and night, answering the phone during supper, and stopping on vacation to make those last three phone calls, but they didn't seem to mind. I always expected someday they would call me with a difficult case and ask for advice due to my vast experience, but I have never received that call. Now my memory is going, so I probably won't have the answer when they do. Through it all, I had a very understanding wife. When I went into intensive care for my second heart surgery, she had all my shoes half-soled. Now there's a real optimist.

≈

 R︎ *Be yourself. Don't try to be somebody else, follow your own ideals. And don't addict more than one patient at a time. Be very sparing in your prescription writing; for nonterminal illness, medication can be a two-edged sword. And if there's any failing in American medicine, it's the failure of preventive medicine.*

124

JOHN E. POWER, M.D.
OPHTHALMOLOGY

I am a native Duluthian, born right here at St. Mary's in 1921. I went to Duluth Central, to Northwestern University, and interned at Cook County in Chicago. I took my eye training at the University of Minnesota. My father was an EENT specialist; he was once chief of staff here and practiced in Duluth until 1958 or so. I practiced with him for a couple of years, but when he died, I went into just ophthalmology. I always admired what my father did because he was a very caring person; I liked the way he cared for people.

In 1950, during the Korean War, I joined the Duluth Air National Guard. In 1951, they federalized the guard and I became the first flight surgeon at the Duluth Air Force Base. I went to school at Randolph Field; I told one of my buddies I had time off at Mardi Gras and said, "Fix me up with some dates." Among them was my wife, and three years later we were married.

I started back here in 1955 and practiced in the Plaza until 1986. I miss the people. I think a lot of retired physicians do.

I can think of one particular case, a boy who had Crouzon's disease, which is a facial dysostosis. We had at that time a plastic surgeon who came up from Minneapolis; his name was Dr. Carline. This boy had eye muscle and lid problems. Dr. Carline and I worked on his face together, and it turned out quite well. That was an interesting one.

The posterior chamber intraocular lens was the biggest advance. And all the medicines we didn't have in those days, And the argon laser to treat glaucoma. When I started doing cataract surgery, people had to stay in bed with sandbags alongside their head for two weeks. I don't know how they survived, on their backs like that. And they had those big coke-bottle glasses because we didn't have any intraocular lenses. Their straight-ahead vision was okay, but they couldn't see out of the corners, had to turn their head to each side to see. And we had only silk sutures, which became loose after two or three days. Except for heart surgery, I don't think there is any branch of surgery that has changed as dramatically as ophthalmology.

I'd do it again; I'd have to learn to put up with it, but I'd do it again if I could. I think in the early days, the general populous respected the physician, held us in some esteem. And we spent more time with them, were closer to them. Because of the third-party business, the biggest thing is the destruction of the doctor/patient relationship. And the paperwork, horrendous! I think we're going to have a form of universal care, and I just thank the good Lord that I don't have to have any part of it. When my father and I started out, Miller was a county hospital; and we used to treat lots of people for nothing; we felt it was our duty to do that. Now you can't do anything for nothing.

One of the reasons I quit in 1986 was that I had a cataract patient I wanted to put in the hospital. In order to do that, I had to call a high school girl in St. Paul to get permission and they said, "No, we won't pay for it." I thought, when that happens, it's time for me to quit. I had raised my family,

I'm not going to starve to death, and it's time to smell the roses. I've got kind of an Irish temper anyway, and I just quit.

To start with, retirement is like a vacation. And then you think, when is this vacation going to end and I have to go back to work? And then, as I said, you start missing the people and doing surgery and all of those things. But gradually you get accustomed to your new life.

R_X *I'm sorry you didn't get to practice like I did in the golden years of medicine—when the doctor/patient relationship wasn't destroyed and eroded like it is now. You are going to get all the advantages. The technology is there, but with the technology comes other problems, too. You can keep people alive indefinitely now: When is a person dead? When are they brain dead? You have to face all those problems that we didn't have to face. But no matter how screwed up health care becomes, it's still a very worthwhile thing. You will still get a lot of satisfaction taking care of people. But I'm sorry you couldn't practice when I did, knowing what we know now.*

128

I came from a big family, five kids. My father was in real estate and insurance, and before that he was an appraiser for the Federal Land Bank.

I was the first doctor in my family; I was always going to be a doctor. In my high school yearbook, that's what I put down. I don't know where the idea came from; I guess I just admired our family doctor. I went to medical school in Minnesota, graduated in 1954, did my internship at St. Paul's and St. Joseph's hospitals, then my residency at Minnesota.

I liked pediatrics. I could take what kids did to me, but I couldn't quite take what adults did. I tell the story about a really obese woman when I was an intern. She burped and passed gas simultaneously, and I said to myself: You know, if a kid did that you could excuse them, but there is no excuse for an adult. And I just like kids, I guess that's the basic answer.

In 1957, I came up here out of residency. I was going to take a cardiac residency at the university, but I thought that if I did, I'd never leave. So I found a place with good hunting and fishing and came north. I had a sister living here; that was a factor. I came up and looked at the clinic and thought it looked like my way to practice. And I've never regretted it. I got here just ahead of Henry Reed. My office looked out on the lake, and Henry's looked out on the parking lot. He's never forgiven me for that.

I practiced for thirty-three years. The only reason I quit was that four of the new doctors who came into the clinic were former patients of mine.

I figured it was time to get out. Dr. Reed retired in September, and I retired in May. He's older than I am. And balder.

There were three of us: Bob Bergan, Henry, and me. We worked every third night and third weekend. Made it nice. Before we had freeways, we made house calls. You'd go to 102nd Avenue West and come back home and then go to 130th. Might as well go to the cities. We made a lot of house calls. You'd load your bag the night before with the drugs you were going to give, and you'd make eighteen, nineteen, twenty house calls a weekend. These young guys don't know how easy they've got it. But it's a different world now. They've got a lot more problems, more technology to deal with than we had. We either won it or lost it.

Probably the most interesting case I had was a little nine-year-old girl that came in for a school exam, and I palpated a mass in her abdomen. We took her to St. Luke's and admitted her. P. L. Eckman opened her up, and she had a cancer of the liver. I went to the book, and the only way to cure this thing was to operate on it. I called a specialist, and he took out over two-thirds of her liver. She survived, has three kids today, and she worked for me as an L.P.N. for eight years. She's very happy to show everybody her scars. She's a great gal. That was one you remember. You don't forget that in a hurry.

I made $12,000 my first year, and the next we got a big raise and made $13,000. I don't know if I would do it again. That's a tough question to answer. We were independent; we would make our own decisions and do our own thing. If I could go back just out of med school, I'm sure I would do the pediatric part again because I wouldn't know any better, wouldn't know how nice we had it back in '57 to '70.

The most amazing advance I saw was pediatric bypass surgery. I was the first pediatric pathologist to train at Minnesota. Unfortunately, I could go up and watch Lillehi and Varco operate, then call my wife and tell her what time to have dinner because I knew how long the baby was going to survive. I'd have to go back down and do the autopsy. Those were big times, the real days.

Retiring was really amazingly easy. Two hours after I threw my name tag in the wastebasket, I was retired. I miss the kids and the nurses, but I was ready, and with the regs and paperwork it was getting to be a rat race. It was still fun, but it wasn't as exciting as it used to be. Maybe that's good because as you get older, you don't need all that excitement. I was active in Kiwanis, which kept me out of my wife's hair. You know that's a problem, because your wife doesn't always retire with you.

❧

R℣ *Never stop learning. You've got to keep up if you're going to keep up. That sounds stupid, but it's certainly true. That's my advice.*

132

My father was a dairy farmer, and very education oriented. We all got burned during the dust bowl. If he wanted my brother or me to take over the farm, he didn't say. Poor land makes poor people.

When the war ended, I was a cadet in the army air force. My father packed me up, and I enrolled spring semester at the University of Kansas. I said, "I'm going to take premed; if it doesn't work out, I'll take something else." I liked it. Competition was stiff; you felt guilty if you went to the picture show.

As a student, I really revered internal medicine, so I got an internal medicine residency at the University of Wisconsin-Madison. The internists took care of the children, as well, and I suddenly realized that's where my interests were. Back in Kansas, during my residency, Drs. Harrington and Coll were down recruiting. I said I wasn't interested, but I talked to Dr. Darrow (of Darrow's Solution) and he said "Henry, get up there, it's gorgeous." I came up at Christmas time; the last boat was going out. No one paid any attention to the cold, which terrified me, but I thought it was the most beautiful place I'd seen. I got a letter stating that Dr. Reardon also had some interest in coming here and asking would I mind if they recruited two people? I would absolutely love it. I finished my residency spring of 1957; Dr. Reardon came the first of July. I took two weeks to go home, so he considers himself the senior partner.

I enjoyed practicing with Dr. Reardon. He made thirty-two years very pleasant for me. He liked to golf and I liked to fish. The first year, I think all doctors worry about whether or not they're going to have a practice, and from then on you worry about how you're going to get some time off.

Everybody has a case you wish you'd never seen and cases you've made the right diagnoses on and are pleased. Ralph Eckman asked me to see a kid who had an eosinophil count of over 50 percent but still didn't look that sick, a little anemic, big liver, big spleen. I had recently read an article on visceral migrans, where children get dog worms which then migrate into the liver and spleen and cause an overwhelming allergic reaction. And sure enough, that's what it turned out to be. I was the new pediatrician, and it takes a case like that to become established.

I practiced for thirty-two years, and cardiac surgery and increased antibiotic efficacy were, I think, the most dramatic advances. We had a whole ward of rheumatic fevers all the time in residency, and all of a sudden we didn't have that any more.

My practice went very much as I wanted it to. Reardon and I were the neurologist, the neonatologist, the allergist, everything. And I think we practiced state of the art medicine at that time. As the subspecialties came, we had access to them, and that made it very pleasant.

I don't miss waking up wondering if the kid with the 104 degree fever perforated his ear and now has meningitis. I don't miss phone calls in the middle of the night. I love retirement. I don't know how I had time to practice. There was no void whatsoever. I had a farewell party; I was immediately ready to go.

~

 ℞ *Try to enjoy yourself. You can't be everything to everybody. You have to figure out what your perspective is, what you want to do. I think you're driven harder than we were, I'm not sure you work as hard. Bergan, Reardon, and I stayed until every sick child was seen. There were no emergency room physicians, no place else for them to go. I don't think you enjoy medicine the way we did. We practiced during the golden age: I believe this is true. And don't practice alone. Paper work. Terrible. I can't conceive of somebody going out by themselves to practice.*

136

WILLIAM D. RUDIE, M.D.
FAMILY MEDICINE

I always thought I would be a doctor. Not because my father was, he never put any pressure on me. I just never thought of anything else.

I was born in Duluth, went to school here, lived here all my life. I entered medical school in 1949, did most of my premed here at UMD, graduated in 1953, interned at St. Mary's, and I've been here ever since. My father, Dr. Christensen, and Dr. Grohs were in the office when I joined them, and my dad was still competent and practicing at eighty-four. Historically, doctors had to keep working because they didn't have enough money to retire. My father used to talk about chipping in to bury fourteen doctors who had died and didn't have enough money for a funeral.

Probably mood-altering drugs were the most dramatic things I saw. When I was in premed, over 50 percent of the hospital beds in Minnesota were psychiatric beds in mental institutions, and they couldn't build them fast enough. We took trips to Moose Lake, Cambridge, and Fairbault, and it really was just pathetic. When mood-altering drugs, major tranquilizers, came along—well, we don't have a mental or psychiatric hospital in the state of Minnesota anymore. They're all closed. Now they're managed as outpatients. That's one of the most dramatic things I remember.

When sulfa first came out it was very dramatic. There was a twelve-year-old kid at scout camp the first time I went; sulfa had just come on the market. My father gave me a packet, a topical powder to use in case I had an infection or something. This kid had an infection in his knee; it had been swollen for months, all full of puss, pretty rotten. I told him I had something that would fix it up. I sprinkled the powder on it, and within forty-eight hours it was healed. Just incredible!

My father talked so much about medicine in the early days; he started in 1920. They were setting bones and taking out appendices, but if they had a medical illness, there really wasn't much to offer. With brain tumors, they'd do air encephalograms, do spinal taps, put in some air and let it go up around the brain and then do X rays of the outside of the brain and try to imagine what was going on inside. When CAT scans came out, it was unbelievable.

I remember so many cases. One night at St. Mary's, two people came in with diphtheria, one at one o'clock and one at two and they were both dead by six. I never found a connection between the two, and I never saw another case.

I was on the tenth floor of the Medical Arts, and there was a deck out about thirty feet. One day I had a lady up in stirrups and the speculum in when the window opens up and the window washer comes in and walks through the room and out the door with his pail and squeegee!

I have three kids, but none of them wanted to work the way I had. I remember when they were young: I worked for three weeks without seeing them. You were a doctor. Your patients came first, and your family really came second. Most of the older doctors lived that way. You got close to your patients. You made house calls; you got to know the family. To do something you enjoy and get paid for it is really something.

138

℞ *If you're honest, you don't have to remember what you said. Control your life. It is possible to organize your practice and do it in such a way that it works for you. You don't accomplish anything by running away from things. It's a good profession, and I guess doing something for forty years and enjoying it as much the last day as the first is something. What bothers me is that we are spending enormous amounts of money on very few people. I think society has to address that. We buy one more day or week for people with terminal conditions—it's got to be sorted out.*

140

JOHN M. RUNQUIST, M.D.
FAMILY MEDICINE

My two brothers and I are native Duluthians; I was born here in 1920. I don't know why I decided to become a physician; that is just what I wanted to be. In about ninth grade, I started taking all my courses with the idea of going into medicine. I graduated from Central, then Duluth Junior College, then Macalaster, and then the University of Minnesota. I took my internship in Portland, Oregon, and then after the service I came back to Duluth.

By this time, 1948, I was married and had two children. I started with the West Duluth Clinic and was there for most of my forty-seven years. I charged fifty cents for an office visit and not much more for a house call. And we made lots of them. I suppose in those years I got maybe an hour of sleep a night. That was not good medicine; you had nothing to go on except your feel, sight, smell; the rest of it was all just guesswork. In the office, you can check a blood pressure or check a white count, but not on a house call. And if people saw my car, they'd send their kids over to have me come to their house to take care of somebody sick there.

I did surgery and OB. I got my training through working with other doctors, and then they would okay me for doing it on my own. I was one of the few doctors in Duluth who had those privileges, which I was rather proud of. By doing a little of everything, it made the practice of medicine much more interesting.

The greatest advance? Probably antibiotics. And now that is going down the drain. We're running into organisms that are resistant to everything. That was something we used to worry about, and now it's here. And CAT scans and MRIs are tremendous advances. When you can see a disease process in the soft tissue, that is something.

I remember very distinctly having seven cases of a form of leukemia, seven cases all in a row, all from Proctor. They weren't related at all, half of them were school teachers, all but one died. I had half a dozen consultants and none of us came up with any good answers. And I only saw it again once, in a very close friend who also died.

We all had a great interest in our patients and tried hard. We did everything we could for them. That's one of the things I don't like about what's going on today. It's assumed that you aren't going to do what you should do, so they have to have rules and regulations, which I think is absolutely wrong. If you aren't going to do the best you can for a patient, then you shouldn't be in medicine. Second opinions? We had them back when I first started, and we were much more strict with each other than they are today. We used to have patient review conferences that you'd better attend or you'd be cut to ribbons. You had to be there to defend yourself. They really went into those things in detail.

Oh, I enjoyed medicine. I lived through the golden years of medicine. We made house calls, but we still had a lot of pleasure in what we were doing, particularly when we were successful. And we always aimed high. None of my children followed me into medicine. They were too smart for that.

Retirement is a little bit hard on the ego. All of a sudden you aren't needed. On the other hand, you wonder why you didn't do this before. Trouble is you have to eat after you retire, too. What is it now, fifty-five dollars for an office call? That's ridiculous. Maybe I made a mistake retiring when I did. And of course you miss the companionship of the other doctors. That was one of the nice things about practicing in Duluth. We were all friends.

~

℞ *Go in with another doctor who's had experience, because at first it's scary. And frankly, today I would not go in by myself under any circumstances, handling the insurance and all that stuff. A group practice will be the easiest for anybody starting out. And if you like the business side, go into administration, not medicine. Why anybody wants to be a medical administrator is beyond me, you can't ever do anything right. You can go to a small town, but go in with one of the other fellas or girls. By doing that you're going to split the network and the calls so that you can get off an hour to go to some of the medical meetings. If you get a little time off, take it. None of us are indispensable. Somebody else can do the work just as well.*

144

JOHN B. SANFORD, M.D.
GENERAL SURGERY

My folks were married in 1915 and both lived to be ninety-four. I was number three of four, born in 1926. I was going to be a doctor from the earliest I can remember. Isn't that strange?

My dad didn't even graduate from high school, so he was very supportive. He worked and got all of his kids through the university. The family doctor was the inspiration, just a great guy. I still have the books he gave me when I was a kid. I never did that, never gave gifts to any of my patients.

I never graduated from high school; I dropped out at the end of eleventh grade. It was 1943; I was seventeen, and a friend said that we could take some tests, skip our senior year, and start at the university. By the time we were old enough for the draft, we'd have a year of college, and who knows what difference that will make? It was tempting, so I started at the university on my seventeenth birthday. Then it was like being caught in a revolving door. In the spring, the military offered a test, I took it and started premed my second year of college. A year later, with a good deal more college credits, I started medical school. I was eighteen, I mean it was just nuts. After three years, I was an M.D. That's when I interned at St. Mary's, had my twenty-second birthday there. That just doesn't happen, it was a war-time circumstance. I didn't have time to be a teenager. Just steady school. I would never advise anybody to do it. It's too much.

In the fall, I got word that the clinic was looking for a surgical resident, so I applied, and I got it. From January 1950 until I went to Korea in January 1951, I worked at the clinic in the surgical department, and because of that experience, I was in a MASH unit.

When I came back to Duluth, someone, I don't remember who, said, "We'd like to have you work with us, where do you want to go for your training?" I said, "I'd like to go to the University of Illinois Medical School." In June, I started my residency in Chicago, and while I was there I met this lovely doctor. It was a hospital romance, and we were married a couple of years later. We came back here in July 1957, and we've been here ever since.

I made $1,000 a month my first year at the clinic. My father never earned any money like that. Between 1956 and 1960, we had four children, and two of them have become physicians. The surgical department was outstanding, and I was very proud to be working there.

As far as surgery in general is concerned, I think cardiac surgery was the biggest advance. And on the medical side, the gastroenterologists changed our practice a lot. Gastric bleeding used to be a surgical problem, gallstones, too. I learned well and never cut or injured a common duct. I used to love that kind of work. Now they're removed endoscopically. As far as my own practice, I settled down to what I wanted to do and tried to do it as well as possible.

I remember a case from the summer of 1971: a guy and his pregnant girlfriend were hit by a semi; it ran up over her belly, and they had to back it off of her. She came to St. Mary's emergency room: We got blood ready

146

and took her up, explored her, and found a terrible tear. We sewed her up and put in lots of drains. She was fine, and her baby was okay. I have often wondered whatever became of them.

I talked myself into retirement. At first I missed going to the operating room. Sometimes I wake up at night, and I'm dreaming I'm in surgery. It doesn't bother me, but it's still a part of me.

I'd do it again, but I'd do it differently: I'd specialize. At the end there was a lot of paperwork, but I don't blame the government as much as the insurance companies—what a rotten, dirty bunch they are. They don't care a thing about their patients, just trying to squeeze money out of the system. While I was in, everything was manageable, and the patient came first.

∾

R$_X$ *Always put the patient first. We spend too much of our resources keeping people alive where it isn't best for the patient. I think there are lots worse things than dying. If you really don't have anything definite to offer, then just be willing to talk it over with the patient. Working together and mutual support among doctors is very important. We're all in this together, we've got to support each other. And enjoy it, lighten up a little bit.*

148

LEONARD A. SARVELA, D.D.S.
ORAL SURGERY

I was born here, parents, grandparents. My father was a very successful dentist. My mother came from a strong Catholic family and married the son of a Lutheran minister. It was very unusual. I have one brother and one sister.

When I graduated from dental school, I went with my father, but I knew I wanted to be an oral surgeon. That required another four years of training at Columbia Presbyterian Medical Center in New York. I wasn't sure what I was going to do. I had offers from New York and Florida, but I came here because my family was here. I was only going to stay a short while. That was in 1954, and I stayed until I retired in 1991. I was with Dr. Bettenhausen from 1954 to 1966, and when he died, I continued by myself.

You know, I had a good-sized practice. At one time I had six girls working in my office and the largest single suite in the Medical Arts Building. I really enjoyed my practice. I was busy; I would see forty patients a day. The girls would take care of the rooms, I would walk in, put the patient to sleep, and do the surgery. Then one of the girls would take care of them until they were awake, and I'd walk to the next room and operate. Often we had meetings at 7 A.M. and I would get home at 7 P.M. A lot of weekend work, a lot of night work. But my father trained me; he said, "If you're going to do it, do it right. If you're going to be a success, work at it. I don't want any complaints; if you're going to do well, you have to sacrifice." My philosophy is you only have three things: time, energy, and resources. If you want to be a success, you've got to sacrifice one, two, or three of those. I've been very fortunate.

One of the most dramatic events was anesthesia. I started using Pentothal, a long-acting IV anesthetic, and when the short-acting Brevatol came on the market, I think I was the first one to use it in this area. Then we could do shorter cases on an outpatient basis in the office.

I cared for a number of very bad accidents—multiple facial bones, put them together, a lot of apparatus, wires coming out. Every case is different. I enjoyed the challenge. A lot of hours of work but it was good.

I would do it all again. I had a great experience, enjoyed it very much. I worked very, very hard because I knew that the opportunities were there. I enjoyed the patients, the physicians, and the dentists I related with, and I made a lot of good friends. But things are changing so fast now. When I was in practice, it was really the golden years. Now there's a lot of government intervention—certain things we can do, certain things we can't. You're going to have an accountant or some guy with an M.B.A. who's trying to make the bottom line saying you ought to practice this way. Judging for all the time and education that you have to go through, I don't know if it's worth the effort.

I've enjoyed my retirement. I'm still involved in a lot of things. I'm active in Rotary and in golf. I get up at the same time every day, read three or four papers, financial papers. I still don't have enough hours in the day. I love business. I have investments, and I spend a lot of time with them. I love to travel; I enjoy people and doing things. I think people are fun.

150

I married a girl from Duluth. We had three children; none of them are in the field. We had a great life. A priest friend of mine told me the way to have a happy marriage is to just try to be nice to each other. That covers everything.

~

 ℞ *I find that some people don't think it's necessary to give back. The attitude for some people is I worked for it, it's mine. But the good Lord has been good to me. I always felt I should repay for some of the things He has given me. Because you don't do this alone. I've been blessed. I guess I've always wanted to do the best I can. No short cuts. I didn't care what it takes, weekends, nights. And I'm still that way. Whatever you do, you have to work at it. If you don't put forth your best effort and try to do whatever the best is, I think you're cheating yourself.*

152

My father was in EENT. I'm the nineteenth doctor on our family tree and the end; no others after me. Kids don't go into medicine so much anymore because of all the government stuff. I was born in Maryland but raised in Saginaw, Michigan. I went to school in Michigan, and I interned in Duluth.

I talked to guys who were doctors' sons, and they said, "Don't intern in the town that your dad's practicing in." I was married and had a child, so I was looking for a good program and good housing. We came up here to look, and it was great. We viewed St. Mary's hospital, and it had everything we wanted. The clinic was the opportunity I wanted, to practice with a group. That was the magnet. I spent a year here and then went back to Detroit for my residency. I was only there a few months when the clinic contacted me, so we came right back here in September, and we've been here ever since.

My first year I made $8,000. I think I only did ten or twelve cases that year because I was assisting my two partners in surgery all the time. It was nice for them to have a young guy come in who was fired up and ready to go. After about a year, I asked them to go back to assisting each other, and I went into practice by myself. MaryAnn Nelson was our surgical nurse for thirty years; she and I operated together all the time, and my practice tripled within a year. What I ended up doing was microsurgery, mostly cataracts and glaucoma. I put in the first implant in town in 1975.

When I came here in 1962, in that year I saw three cases of congenital glaucoma. You maybe see two in a whole practice time. What happens is the pressure goes up, and the eye is soft and mobile, so it gets bigger and bigger and bigger, and if you don't do them within the first three months, then they're guaranteed to go blind because the eye can't tolerate that. I did the only goneotomy that's ever been done in this area that I know of.

My first office was just a little cubbyhole, Dr. John Winter's old office. My office and exam room were the same, five feet wide and twelve feet long, and I divided the exam room in half and made two out of it. The clinic was very accommodating, made a point of having every piece of equipment that you wanted.

The biggest advance was the implantable lens, no question about it. Revolutionized not only the surgery but the outcomes and the morbidity. People used to have to go in the hospital for a week and then recuperate for six weeks. Big fat glasses, couldn't see for beans. Sick to their stomach, they were in terrible shape. And then we'd do the surgery and at the same time put the implant in, and they'd wake up and see 20/20. Now we do them in outpatient surgery. I did about five thousand. It's amazing. It was undoubtedly the biggest revolution in eye surgery that ever came along.

I've enjoyed retirement, yes, absolutely. The secret is to have enough interests going on before you ever retire. Kay and I went to Costa Rica with Elderhostel in Duluth. That was really great, lots of fun. Last summer and most of the fall, I worked for Habitat for Humanity, building houses.

I would be very skeptical about going into medicine again—too much interference. That's why I got out; I was fortunate enough to have reached the point where I could do it. But the last two years with this new Minnesota Care thing, terrible. Optometrist therapeutic drug bill, terrible, Overhauling all of the medical system, kill the goose and start over, terrible. Canadian system, worse than terrible.

~

R℞ *For a young person going into medicine the problem is going to be that you'll take all the risks to get through school and come out with a big debt. You can't make the debt, can't pay it off because your fees are fixed, and what you can do is fixed so you don't have control of your practice anymore. They've created these Medicare review boards and a huge bureaucracy to go with it, and pretty soon, if you're going to do a case under them, you're losing money. Not only are you losing money, but they sent me notices that they reviewed three charts and refused payment. I challenged, and I found out that the reviewers were high school kids, that's where they work. I just said, "That's it." I didn't go to school to have a high school kid telling me what I can do. That's what's going to happen with the Medicare system. Bad news.*

156

KENNETH A. STORSTEEN, M.D.
GENERAL SURGERY

I sort of drifted into medicine. The one doctor in our local hospital influenced me to go into medicine; I guess that's why I chose it. My parents were careful not to influence us. They let us decide what we wanted. They encouraged me once I decided to go into medicine, but they didn't force me.

I was born in Webster, South Dakota, in 1920. I went to Augustana College, then into the military, and wherever I went in the service, they all seemed to talk about the Mayo Clinic, all good reports. So I took my training there. My wife and I had taken a trip up to Lake Kabetogama the year before I was going to leave Mayo. We really liked the woods and water, and we had relatives who had done a lot of canoeing up here and always talked about it.

Dr. Thomas Young needed a younger surgeon to help out; he offered me a job, so I decided that Duluth was a good place.

I came here in 1954 and practiced with Dr. Young for twenty years. After he died, we had a five-man general surgery group: Dr. Swensen first, then Dr. Cuderman, Dr. Barbee, Dr. Nevonen, and then I retired in February 1988. I was chief of surgery at St. Mary's, St. Luke's, and Miller Dwan, and I did general surgery at all three.

There were a couple of developments that really made a difference to surgeons. The use of flexible scopes, the development of endoscopy, was a major one, probably the most important. Helped a lot in the management of gastrointestinal and colonic troubles. The second most important thing was the development of vascular surgery to the point where disease could be corrected in a higher percentage of cases.

Once I did a liver resection on an eight-month-old baby girl; she had a huge tumor. I was able to resect it, and she had no recurrence. I saw her as an adult; the liver had regenerated; she was healthy, and she was going to have a baby. That was interesting—there wasn't much liver resection done before that time. I saw some bad trauma cases. One of them, a ten-year-old boy, was run over by a truck. His leg was numb and cold, and he had a rupture of an iliac artery. I took a vein graft from the opposite leg and put it in there because the ends were so far apart. He did just fine. There were some major pancreatic surgeries, pancreatectomies, that were very gratifying.

We didn't have sophisticated measuring devices for monitoring people, but I think the doctors were more personable in the early days, a little more friendly to the patient than they are now. Now it's strictly business. Maybe it's for the best, but I think patients received good care in those days.

I missed the camaraderie with the doctors for six months. After that I got used to being away, and then I enjoyed it. Some days I just sit and look at the lake. But I have plenty of work here, gardening with all the land we have, about eight acres, and I do a lot of hunting and fishing and golfing. I have Parkinson's disease; I get along with it pretty well, but my wife claims I'm a little slow, and that's to be expected. You do the best you can. Oh yes, I'd do it again. I enjoyed it, especially the patient contact. It was fun to sit down and talk to people. We have four adopted children, and none of them went into medicine. My daughter said I was not home very much. She said that. I think she meant it. I would get up at six thirty and get to the hospital by seven thirty. It seemed every minute I did before eight o'clock was worth two minutes afterwards. You just got going a little bit better. You'd have to see your post-ops; you'd see all the people in the office and then go to the hospital and make rounds, especially the critically ill ones, ones that you'd operated on. So then you'd get home about nine o'clock. I remember one lady I was going to do a thyroidectomy on. I came to see her at ten at night and she said, "Young man, you get home and get some sleep. You're operating on me tomorrow." That was a good one! But I would certainly do it over again, sure. Every little challenge was gratifying. I especially liked surgery because you could find something wrong, repair it, and they got well.

❧

R︁x *Work hard and apply what you've learned. The most important thing is patient care. Let the patient know that you are available. Don't be away from your practice too long, and don't try to exclude yourself from work. Be available. Of course, you've got to be kind to your patient; understand and listen. Let the patient do some talking. Don't be too quick to leave, because they want to talk. That's most of it.*

160

JOHN M. STREITZ, M.D.
UROLOGY

I chose urology because my friend Malcolm Fifield, who I met in medical school, was in it, and he thought it was great. I have known him just short of fifty years, and we practiced together for thirty-four, until he retired. We decided we'd practice in a place where we could have a sailboat, this is to say a REAL boat, and we ended up in Duluth. I graduated from the University of Minnesota, and I started my practice here in 1955. Dr. Brooker was a general practitioner, obviously destined to be a surgeon, and he joined us in 1962. We were a compatible group, and Duluth was a good place for us. Dr. Hutchens joined us twenty years ago, time goes by fast. I feel like a native now. People wondered why we were leaving the city to go to Duluth. I wonder about people staying there—why do they?

I remember a man who had cancer of the kidney. In 1955, it wasn't appreciated how frequently tumors grew down the renal vein and into the vena cava. We stumbled onto one of those, and we got a tear in the vena cava. The priest was in the operating room giving the last rites to the patient, and that made a big impression on Dr. Fifield. We called a surgeon, John Thomas. The three of us got him fixed up, and the man did just fine. Twenty-five years later, he got a cancer of the colon, and this cancer obstructed his left ureter. One of my partners, in my absence, reimplanted the right ureter, where there was now no kidney, over to the left side, and this man lived another two years. Nowadays, one would never be surprised to find a tumor because diagnostically we can pick it up ahead of time. But at that time there was no way to do it.

The development of the CT scan was most significant; the MRI was also. But in urology, specifically it was the development of tiny flexible scopes so that we could go up the ureter into the kidney and extract stones. And the extracorporeal lithotripter as well—the ability to break up kidney stones without invasion using shock waves—it's made kidney surgery so rare that residents have a hard time getting experience the way we did. They now explore very few kidneys, and that was an everyday thing when I was a resident.

I have five children, and three of them are physicians. None of them were pushed into it, I guess they just liked what they saw. Oh yes, I'd do it again. People talk about the difficulties of practicing today. The entry level is what it is when you come on the scene. If kids have never known anything different, then the way medicine is today doesn't seem onerous.

Retirement was just fine. I had been thinking about it for a year or more, so it was easy. Thirty-seven years is long enough. I think you tend to get stale after awhile. Getting up in the middle of the night to operate had lost its charm the last few years. I don't miss that at all.

R_x *Remember that you have to talk to, listen to, and then examine the patient. All required modern diagnostic tests are supplemental to that and always should be. If you skip the old history and physical you're going to go wrong. I think medicine is practiced better today; treatment is more standardized; there are norms. Once you have a diagnosis there isn't a lot of leeway in terms of what you're going to do. Twenty years ago, diagnostics were not that specific; there were a lot of ideas about treatment. There's a great story about an autocratic surgeon who said, "Mrs. Jones, you're going into the hospital for surgery." And she said, "Dr., what are you going to do?" He said, "Never mind, that doesn't involve you at all." Today I think patients get a fairer shake in terms of explanation. You sit down, explain the risks and complications, what you're going to do, and the alternatives.*

164

I was born in Duluth in 1921. I went to Central, then to junior college, and graduated from medical school in 1946. I knew I was pointing to be a doctor in high school. Both of my parents were very encouraging and supportive.

My wife and I grew up together. We were married when I finished medical school. I served two years in Japan and came back to the States in 1949. I finished my surgical residency in 1953 and came here in 1954. I came by myself, and I stayed by myself in the Medical Arts Building until I retired.

The biggest difference in operating rooms then and now was lighting. We had one central bulb that had fixed mirrors and glass ports that were prefocused to bring the light down to the field. It's what you grew up with.

We depended on curare for relaxation, which was very difficult and short. You'd be working in a belly, which is where I spent most of my time, and the patient would start waking up. It was a struggle to finish. Children's anesthesia was open drop ether, and we used it for adults, too. The cone fit over the patient's face, and the anesthesiologist poured it out of a can, drop by drop. But that's an era that is completely gone.

It was difficult getting started here, being a general surgeon. I did a lot of things to make a living. I served as physician for the county jail and work farm for several years. There was no trained surgeon in Superior, so when two young men opened a general practice, they asked me to come over and do some of their surgery. They were intent on keeping the practice in Superior at St. Mary's and St. Joe's. I was over there a couple times a week for several years. I was very fortunate. It kept me alive.

I had five children, I didn't encourage any of them to become doctors. They are all quite self-sufficient and made their own decisions.

The polio vaccine made a dramatic change. And the advent of antibiotics to treat infectious disease. Penicillin was so expensive and hard to get. It is excreted in the urine, and they were collecting urine from patients and re-extracting the penicillin, that was how difficult it was.

The intensive care units made a huge difference, concentrating the care of patients in a particular area. Pre-operative preparation of patients and postanesthesia recovery rooms were also important along with appreciation of the significance of blood loss. Surgeons would get the work done and make up for blood loss later. Modern surgeons appreciate that blood loss is expensive to the patient. Surgeons remember their failings. At least I do. The times you failed, they stay with you. They run through your mind in those quiet hours when you're trying to sleep. That's when the devil has come . . . the devils.

The clinic had trained surgeons, but Duluth didn't have many. Storsteen came first, then Bob Goldish, then I came, then Fifield, then Streitz. There were several of us, out of residency programs and various specialties, and as a group we made quite an impact on the way medicine was practiced here.

166

I remember a case that Fifield and Streitz did, a patient with a huge kidney tumor growing into the vena cava and a tremendous amount of blood loss. I was in the office, and they called and said can you come up and help us. When I got there, they had stopped the anesthesia because the patient didn't have any blood pressure. Between the three of us, we sewed up that hole in the vena cava and restored blood volume, and he survived. That was a good day—one of those days when you're very lucky.

The first year of retirement was very difficult. The paperwork was an unacceptable burden, and I didn't miss that at all. What I missed was seeing my friends, other physicians, nursing staff, administrative staff—familiar faces and the usual exchange between people who work together all day. I missed being in the operating room. I still do. If we did all the rest of the foolishness, going to the operating room was the reward.

I had a very good experience, very stimulating, exciting. I had fun. I enjoyed all of it—creating a practice, a routine in the office. Janice was with me for twenty-five years, a jewel. I was very fortunate.

~

R̠x *Remember that the needs of the patients come first.*

168

NOEL E. TOSSELAND, M.D.
GENERAL SURGERY

My folks lived in southern Minnesota. Our little town had a doctor but no medical facilities so my mother went home to Sioux City, Iowa, to have me. I'm an Iowan by birth but I've lived in Minnesota all my life. I'm an only child; my father was an educator, superintendent of public schools in southern Minnesota.

I hadn't decided to go into medicine until I was nearly through St. Olaf College. I applied at the University of Minnesota, as well as several other schools, but the U lost my application and said I could reapply the next year. St. Louis University in Missouri was the first response I got, and it was a good school, so I took it to have somewhere to go that year. Once I went, I stayed and finished medical school in St. Louis. I was expecting to go into the service after my internship at St. Mary's, but they turned me down—I'd had a thyroidectomy and had a visual defect. So I applied for a surgical fellowship at the Mayo Clinic, and I was accepted. After I was there a year, they decided they wanted me after all, and I went into the army.

After the service I was accepted back at the Mayo Clinic, finished a little more than two years, so I had good surgical fellowship there. I decided that if I was going to start out on my own, I might as well go back to the Duluth area. I opened my office in the Medical Arts Building in 1949 and just waited until somebody came. Had to borrow enough money to pay rent for both our house and the office, but we happened to own a car.

I listed myself as a general surgeon, but many other things came along. One day, one of the nuns stopped me in the hall and said, "Dr. Tosseland, you're early on in your practice, you're not too busy, are you?" I said "Well, not yet." She said, "Do you think you could run our health service for us?" I said I'd see what I could do, and I set up the health service at St. Mary's in 1952. In 1956 Dr. Varney wanted to retire, and he came to me and said, "You know, if you want it, you could be the examining doctor for the Pittsburgh fleet, and you'll also get the contract for the U.S. Public Health Service." I said I ought to be able to handle it. It is slow going for a long while when you're on your own. I made $75 my first month in practice, but that was a long time ago. I didn't worry about it, one thing or another came along. Then the VA contacted me; they wanted to have additional exams done in Superior, and I said I could do that one day a week. I handled a lot of different people. Working with the seamen, I saw everything.

One time a seaman came in with typhoid fever, almost never heard of around here, but we had one—stirred up the whole country. And I had a man who was brought into the ER almost cut in half by a hawser. When the ship moved it snapped and cut him right through the middle. They called me and said, "You have a man here that's bleeding to death." I got there as soon as I could, and I asked them to call Jim Monge. When he got there, I'd already been clamping bleeders for fifteen or twenty minutes, and I'd finally stopped the flow of blood. We got him put together, but he needed twenty-four units of blood, and then he got gangrene. We sent him to the VA to the decompression chamber; they operated again in the chamber, but he finally died. That was the most severe injury I ever saw that was still alive when I first saw him.

Penicillin came in about the time I was an intern, but it was mostly sulfa even then. I would say that the advent of antibiotics changed medicine more than anything else. And changed surgery, too. And then the advances in vascular surgery, being able to reconstruct arteries that were cut off or plugged, and then that led to open heart surgery.

I had planned on retirement for so long. When I got to be sixty-five, I was going to quit. I was never going to get to the point that somebody would tell me I shouldn't be working. For me, it worked fine because we got involved shortly thereafter in our place in Arizona.

We have three children; none of them became doctors. As of now, starting over, I doubt that I would do it. I couldn't possibly think of it, it would be a different world.

≈

 R_x *My era is gone. I don't believe my kind of practice will ever exist again. There will be private practitioners, but there will never be someone who can practice as a general surgeon, by himself. You have to work in a group in some way. I've probably seen the best of medicine, with everything that's happened.*

172

PAUL S. VANPUFFELEN, M.D.
ORTHOPEDICS

My father was a Presbyterian minister in charge of a mission school in Brussels, Belgium, when I was born in 1929. I lived there until the first grade, and then we came back to the States. Following that, my sister was born; my father had one church after another, and we moved around a lot. We moved to Minnesota in 1946 and stayed. I went to Wheaton College and then to the University of Minnesota Medical School. When I started looking for internships, several people spoke so highly of the medical care in Duluth and the hospitals they interned at up here, I thought I'd go up and take a look. I graduated in 1957 and interned at St. Luke's 1957–58. I went into general practice with Henry Geronimus for two years, and then I decided I wanted to go into orthopedic surgery, so I spent four years in the Mayo Clinic program.

Then we took a trip to the Southwest, thought we might be interested in going there. But the opportunities I had in Duluth were much better than at any of the other places that I looked.

My wife and I were married the week before I started my internship, and we have two boys and a girl.

When I came back, I started working with Dr. William Zwebart. Not too long after, Dr. Heisel joined us and then Dr. Gower, and we kept building the group to about six. I started working in 1957 and retired December 1989.

In orthopedics, the beginning of doing total joint replacements was probably the biggest change. We started out with total hips and then subsequently total knees. I did the first total knee in town at St. Mary's. Starting out with completely new procedures that had never been done before was a real challenge. They really made a big difference in the number of people that were otherwise crippled because of their pain. The biggest problem I see is the results are so good that people aren't willing to go along with a conservative approach, and I've always been very conservative. Two things I always emphasize are: first, make sure you're having surgery because you need it, and second, try everything else first. In the hands of a conservative orthopedist, the end results and patient satisfaction level is going to be higher.

It's interesting that you ask about complicated cases because a year ago I spent a month in St. Lucia, and they brought in a five-year-old girl who had been running a temperature of 106 degrees for a week. She was toxic, and her left leg was swollen all the way down. I took her to the OR, aspirated a couple of spots, and found frank pus in her ankle. We washed it out, put her on antibiotics, and she got worse. I told her mother I would have to take her back, and she said, "No, we're taking her home," which was what the voodoo doctor from their village had recommended. I said, "If you take her, she's going to die." They finally agreed to see the black doctor who was with us. It took him two hours, but we took her back. I aspirated her calf and found a huge abscess. A medical student from Loyola

174

had brought some Rocephin with him, and basically that saved this child's life. It was really a lot of satisfaction.

I play golf all the time in the summer, and I ski all winter. We're traveling a lot, and these volunteer stints for a month at a time are things I couldn't do when I was in practice. I didn't realize that I was under as much tension and pressure as I was. Really sort of thrived on it, I guess. I thought I would miss the surgery more than I have. The things I miss most are the people that I worked with. Because you build up lifelong friendships there.

I'd do it all again, the same way. I was going to be a doctor from early high school. I never even thought about doing anything else. I feel really good about the whole experience.

∾

 ℞ *Over the years, the three things I've felt strongly about are first, you've got to treat patients like people in a sympathetic, kind way. Secondly, you must build a relationship with the people working with and for you. I always enjoyed it, and the only way you can do that is by being nice to them and respecting them. Third, never do anything in medicine with the thought of how much money you're going to get from it. People concerned about money have their priorities turned around.*